Teacher's
MANUAL

to

The Odyssey
retold by Robin Lister

By Ann Maouyo

Talent Development Secondary Publications
Center for Social Organization of Schools
Johns Hopkins University
Baltimore

Table of Contents

TALENT DEVELOPMENT SECONDARY (TDS)

ENGLISH LANGUAGE ARTS DIVISION

MISSION STATEMENT

RESPONDING TO THE CHANGING NATURE OF LITERACY BY PROVIDING STUDENTS WITH SKILLS THAT WILL ENDURE BEYOND THE CLASSROOM

Student Team Literature Discussion Guides are designed to support teachers with organizing literacy instruction to respond to the needs of diverse student populations while striving to meet the growing instructional demands of state and district college- and career-readiness standards.

Using whole-class structures, peer discussion, and teacher modeling, this instructional framework affords students regular opportunities to engage in oral language, critical analysis and exploration of information extending to real world applications. Students intuitively deepen understanding of content and develop their inferring and evidence-gathering skills through ongoing exposure to inductive learning, a powerful strategy underlying higher-order thinking and 21st century skills. Teachers routinely facilitate small-group and whole-class discussions to help students apply academic language and develop new insights and perspectives as they read various types of authentic texts. Teachers are also encouraged and equipped to use a variety of informational texts in conjunction with literary works, and to provide students with the skills they need to comprehend these increasingly complex texts. Through reading and writing for different purposes and from multiple perspectives, students move toward the self-regulated learning and independent thinking required to function in today's society.

In the midst of the flow of information surrounding adolescent literacy, we recognize the significant role that motivation plays in the lives of adolescent learners. The instructional design and materials used in the TDS program enable students to exercise mental processes needed to comprehend, communicate, reason, evaluate, and persevere. Students take ownership of learning experiences and make choices within a responsive, student-centered classroom environment.

With the growing demands of the 21st century, the TDS ELA Discussion Guides offer flexibility and guidance to teachers who seek specific focus and clarity when planning instruction. Teachers are able to build instructional modules around core reading selections using existing approaches and activities contained in the Discussion Guides. This approach helps establish historical and factual connections, and addresses specific assessments, standards and skills in the context of teaching the core reading selections. Using this method to planning and teaching literacy, classroom teachers and TDS instructional support staff can effectively collaborate around core approaches to promote achievement for all students in the 21st century.

To the Teacher

This Teacher's Manual is part of a research-based, cooperative approach to teaching literature developed by the Talent Development Secondary Program at the Johns Hopkins University. This approach, called Student Team Literature, strengthens students' thinking, reading, writing, and social skills. In Student Team Literature, students read quality books and work in learning teams using *Student Discussion Guides* that lead them to become critical thinkers, expand their working vocabularies, and broaden their knowledge of the writer's craft. Guides are available to support study of over 70 novels, biographies, and short story and poetry collections. Students read the literature and work through a Student Discussion Guide using a weekly cycle of instruction.

Each Student Discussion Guide includes the following components:

- **Vocabulary Lists** expose students to terms they need to know in order to understand what they are reading.

- **Starred High Frequency Words** are those that students acquire for their working vocabularies, as they occur often in many contexts. Students learn to use these words in meaningful sentences that include context clues to show understanding of the new words.

- **Writer's Craft Boxes** provide information about aspects of the writer's craft (e.g., flashbacks, figurative language) that students encounter in the literature. Craft Boxes can be used as the basis for mini-lessons.

- **Questions** and **Graphic Organizers** lead students to analyze the literature, organize information, and better understand the writer's message.

- **Make a Prediction** and **What If? Boxes** lead students to establish expectations about what will come next in their reading.

- **Selection Review** questions and answers are used by pairs of students to prepare for literature tests.

- **Literature-related Writing** suggestions lead students to respond to literature and try various forms of writing.

- **Extension Activities** give students opportunities to express themselves in response to the text through art, drama, research, and other activities.

- **So, You Want to Read More...** suggests books for independent reading that match the one students have read in theme, genre, or topic.

- **About the Author** provides biographical information, as well as listing some of the writer's other works.

In addition to these sections, each Teacher's Manual also includes:

- a **Summary** of the book or literary work

- a **Building Background** section with suggestions for preparing students to read the literary work

- a **Preview/Predict/Purpose** section with questions that lead students to establish expectations before beginning to read

- **Guided Discussion** questions and suggestions for whole-class discussions

- **Listening Comprehension/Read Aloud Connections** identifying relevant literary elements and devices and listing short works that include these features, which teachers can use to prepare and present *Listening Comprehension* lessons (a teacher read-aloud/think-aloud activity that serves as a companion to Student Team Literature)

These materials can be used within or outside the context of the Student Team Literature program, although we believe teachers who have been trained in the program make the best use of them. (Please see below for teacher training contact information.)

About the Literature

The most effective motivation for adolescent readers lies in the relevance of the literature they are presented. Poor or reluctant readers are particularly in need of relevance in the written word. They need to see themselves in the pages they turn.

Today's adolescents are fortunate; never have they had so much quality literature available that reflects their experiences, their problems, and their cultures. The driving force behind Student Team Literature is making accessible the best of middle grades literature. Discussion Guides have been written for a wide variety of literary works at every readability level, from high interest/low readability selections to classic literature used in middle grades English language arts instruction for over twenty-five years.

The Weekly Instruction Cycle

Discussion Guides enable teachers to lead learning teams through literary works in a cycle of activities that includes **direct instruction**, **team practice and discussion**, and **individual assessment**. After careful preliminary vocabulary instruction, students: (1) read a selected text portion silently; (2) complete (optional) Partner Reading, which gives poor readers and second language learners additional practice to build fluency by reading excerpts aloud; (3) discuss with their partners possible responses to questions and activities in Student Discussion Guides; and, (4) write individual responses to the questions and activities.

Discussion Guides and Cooperative Learning

Discussion Guides are designed to be used in the classroom in the context of cooperative learning. Cooperative learning requires students to learn and exercise many social and academic skills, beginning with the most basic, such as active listening and staying on task. For that reason, introducing students (and teachers, during professional development) to Student Team Literature typically involves direct instruction in relevant skills. The teacher determines the skills to be taught (one at a time), the order in which they will be introduced, and students' readiness to add new skills. Instruction includes discussion of the skill and its importance; completion of a T-chart to show what the skill looks and sounds like (making abstract social skills more concrete for students); and modeling and role-playing use of the skill. As students apply the skills in daily classroom activities, teachers monitor and reinforce their use. Students gradually internalize the skills, creating a cooperative learning climate that has an important positive impact on classroom management and academic achievement.

Assessment

Three assessment tools are available to teachers who use Student Team Literature guides. Each week, after quizzing each other in a process called "Selection Review," students take **literature tests** that require short constructed responses. **Vocabulary tests** assess students' ability to compose meaningful sentences using the high frequency words they have studied in the context of the literature. These Selection Reviews, literature tests, and vocabulary tests are provided on reproducible pages at the end of each Teacher's Manual. In addition, students can practice their standardized test taking skills in relation to the literary work they have studied by taking Standardized Reading Practice Tests that are similar in format to the standardized tests used in school districts throughout the country. Standardized Reading Practice Tests must be ordered separately.

Ordering information

The Talent Development Secondary program offers Teacher's Manuals, Student Discussion Guides, and a Standardized Reading Practice Test booklet including reproducible assessment pages.

- To place an order, call 410-516-4339 or email tds@jhu.edu. The complete Talent Development Secondary materials catalog is available online on our website (see below).

- For teacher training or more on our English language arts, math, science, or social studies programs, contact Maria Waltemeyer at 410-516-2247 or mwaltemeyer@jhu.edu

- Also visit our website at
    www.talentdevelopmentsecondary.com/curriculum

About
The Author

The *Odyssey* was probably written around 750 B.C. as a sequel to another ancient Greek epic poem, the *Iliad*, the fictionalized account of the Greeks' war against the city of Troy several hundred years earlier. According to tradition, a blind poet named Homer composed both poems, but we know practically nothing about Homer himself. Some scholars wonder whether Homer even existed, and whether the *Iliad* and the *Odyssey* were composed by the same poet or by different poets. One reason we are not very sure is that both poems probably began as oral traditions: professional singers passed them along by word of mouth long before anyone wrote them down. Homer may have collected the traditional songs about Odysseus,

continued...

The Odyssey

Retold by Robin Lister

TEACHER'S MANUAL
Suggested length of time to be spent on this book: 3 weeks

Summary

This version of the *Odyssey* is a retelling in prose of the classic Greek epic poem by Homer. In this retelling, the story begins with Odysseus (Oh-DISS-ee-us), once lord of the kingdom of Ithaca, being blown away from the shores of his island home just as he was arriving, by the angry sea god Poseidon (Poh-SIDE-un). He shipwrecks on a distant shore, where Nausicaa (NAW-sick-uh), daughter of the Phaiaecian (Fy-EE-shun) king, finds him and leads him to her father's court. A court musician sings the song of the Greeks' long conflict with the city of Troy—a conflict won at the cost of many lives and great heartbreak. Afterward, Odysseus, commander of the ill-fated Greek army, takes up the story where the musician left off. In the chapters that follow, he recounts how horrible monsters threatened and beautiful women detained him, and describes sites that range from an island paradise to the underworld itself. He has been unable to return home for a full ten years since the end of the war, which itself lasted ten long years. When his tale is over, the Phaiaecian king, himself a descendant of Poseidon, promises to send Odysseus home safely at last. However, when Odysseus arrives in Ithaca, he faces a new challenge. Because of his long absence, suitors are pressing around his wife Penelope (Pen-ELL-oh-pey), eager to acquire his fortune and title. With the help of the goddess Athena, Odysseus enters the court disguised as a beggar. He takes his grown son Telemachus (Tuh-LEM-uh-kus) into his confidence, and challenges the suitors to a contest for Penelope's hand. Of course, Odysseus is the victor; he and Telemachus clear the house of the unwanted interlopers, and Odysseus reveals his true identity to the faithful Penelope.

Building Background

Ask students to find the Mediterranean Sea on a globe or world map. Provide a large, wall-size map of the Mediterranean world (either ancient or modern will do). Locate Greece, and find Odysseus' island

polished them, and had them written down as one long story. Or, perhaps he made up the tales of the *Odyssey* and taught them to disciples or followers who learned them by heart, then wrote them down at a later date. We simply do not know for sure.

home, Ithaca (located on the western coast of Greece, about 38.5° N latitude and 20.5° E longitude, designated "Ithaki" on modern maps). Also, locate the site of Troy, in northeastern modern-day Turkey (about 40° N latitude and 26° E longitude).

Explain to students that ancient Greece was not a single nation, but a group of tiny kingdoms, which later became the Greek city-states. The small kingdoms united from time to time in response to crisis situations. For example, the Trojan War, which forms the background of the *Odyssey*, was said to have begun when the king of Sparta appealed to the other Greek kings to help him recover his wife Helen from Paris, the prince of Troy, with whom she had eloped. (Modern-day scholars suspect that the Greeks' ambition to control the strategic waterway linking the Caspian and Mediterranean Seas was probably the real motive.) Archaeologists have determined that the city of Troy really did exist—and have found the remains of no less than nine successive cities on the site of Troy. The seventh city burned to the ground around 1200 B.C., probably in the course of the conflict we know today as the Trojan War.

Explain to students that, while the story of the Trojan War is at least partially historic, the subsequent legends found in the *Odyssey* are almost entirely imaginative fantasy. We cannot identify many of the places mentioned in the story with any accuracy. The stories are also deeply rooted in Greek mythology. Invite students to recall what they may have learned about Greek mythology in previous classes. Remind them that the king of the Greek gods was Zeus (ZOOSS), the god of the sky. Most other principal gods were either Zeus's brothers and sisters—such as Poseidon, the god of the sea, and Hades (HAY-deez), the god of the underworld— or his children, for example, Athena (Uh-THEE-nuh), the goddess of wisdom; Aphrodite (Af- ro-DIE-tey), the goddess of love; Apollo (Uh-PAH-loh), the god of the sun; and Ares (AIR-eez), the god of war. In addition to these, there were a vast number of lesser gods, monsters, and heroes, some of them even older than Zeus himself.

The Greeks believed that these gods and goddesses, though much more powerful than human beings, were not all-powerful, and certainly not always wise or good. They were subject to jealousies, passions, and trickeries on a super-human scale. They also inter-vened quite directly in human life, and much of the tension of the *Odyssey* comes from Odysseus' attempts to get around the oppo-sition of certain gods or goddesses with the help of other more favorable ones.

Want To Read More

If you enjoyed reading the *Odyssey*, you might want to read other retellings of ancient mythology, such as Penelope Lively's *In Search of a Homeland: the Story of the Aeneid*, *D'Aulaire's Book of Greek Myths*, by Ingri and Edgar Parin D'Aulaire, or Mary Pope Osborne's *Favorite Greek Myths*. You might also like to read non-fiction works about the ancient world, such as Virginia Schomp's *The Ancient Greeks* or Andrew Solway's *Ancient Greece*. Or, you might like to read retellings of other well-known legends, such as Robin Lister's *The Story of King Arthur*, J. Walter McSpadden's *Robin Hood* or Robin McKinley's *The Outlaws of Sherwood*.

Briefly review the Roman numeral system, since chapter numbers in the book are given in Roman numerals.

Listening Comprehension/Read Aloud Connections

The *Odyssey* in its original form was an epic poem. Introduce your students to the concept of **epic** by reading Tessa Potter's *Beowulf and the Dragon* or Robert Sabuda's *Arthur and the Sword*.

Story-within-a-story is a device used often in the *Odyssey;* examples are found in Kate Duke's *Aunt Isabel Tells a Good One*, Thomas Locker's *The Boy Who Held Back the Sea*, and Ann Grifalconi's *The Village of Round and Square Houses* (which is an example of **myth** as well).

Introduce students to the ***in medias res*** device used here by reading Byrd Baylor's *One Small Blue Bead* or Steven Kellogg's *The Mystery of the Missing Red Mitten*. Or, try reading a "drama in real life" story from a popular magazine such as *The Reader's Digest*; such stories almost invariably use this device.

The *Odyssey* contains a number of **ironies**. For examples of irony, read David Small's *Imogene's Antlers* or John Steptoe's *Mufaro's Beautiful Daughters*. Or read Chris Van Allsburg's *The Sweetest Fig*, or O. Henry's well-known short story, "The Gift of the Magi."

Examples of **metaphor** and **personification**, which are frequent in the *Odyssey,* can be found in Lyn Littlefield Hoopes' *The Unbeatable Bread* and Joyce Carol Thomas' *I Have Heard of a Land*.

To focus on basic **plot elements**, including **complications**, **climax**, and **dénouement,** read Bernard Waber's *Ira Sleeps Over*, Kate Duke's *Aunt Isabel Tells A Good One*, William Hooks' *Moss Gown*, or Steven Kellogg's *Ralph's Secret Weapon*.

Symbolism is important in the *Odyssey*; good examples abound in Alice Walker's *Finding the Green Stone*, Margery Williams' *The Velveteen Rabbit*, or some of Dr. Seuss' more thoughtful works, such as *The Lorax; Horton Hatches the Egg; Horton Hears a Who; The Sneetches and Other Stories*; or *Yertle the Turtle and Other Stories*.

Preview/Predict/Purpose

Tell students that the *Odyssey* is a story about why it took Odysseus, the king of the island of Ithaca, ten more years to reach his home after he had finished ten years of war against the city of Troy, a little over two hundred miles away. It also tells the story of the challenges that met him when he finally did arrive home after twenty years of absence.Have students **preview** the book by looking at the front and back covers. Ask them to comment on the images and description.

Have students **predict** some of the problems that might prevent Odysseus from returning home for ten years after the war's end. Ask them to **predict** what might have become of his wife and young son when he finally reaches home.

Invite students to set a **purpose** for reading. They might want to learn some of the ancient stories that form the background for Western civilization today. They might want to compare Odysseus' adventures and misadventures with the perils faced by modern heroes in epic movies and video games. They might want to think about the life lessons to be learned from Odysseus' experience.

Discussion Guide #1

Chapters 1 - 5 (pages 1-29)

Write the starred words from the **VOCABULARY LIST** on the next page and their definitions on chart paper or sentence strips that will remain posted throughout the time that students work on the Discussion Guide.

Prepare a **Vocabulary Prediction Chart** (see illustration below) for students to complete after you have introduced the reading selection and the **VOCABULARY LIST**, and before they have begun to read. The chart contains categories into which starred words from the list are to be placed. Students predict how each starred word relates to the reading selection, or if it is impossible to predict its relationship. Categories can be adjusted according to the type of literature being read.

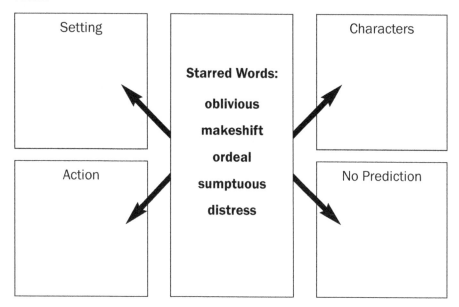

First, read aloud the list of words in the order in which they appear. Second, reread the words and have students repeat each one after you. Third, ask students if they know the definitions of any of the words. Confirm correct definitions, or, in the case of multiple-meaning words, identify definitions that match the context in which the words are used in the poems. Next, ask students if they recognize parts of unfamiliar words. If students' decoding skills are below level, stress at this time the sounds of syllables — especially in starred words. In all cases, use this time to focus on identifying the meanings of any prefixes, suffixes or roots that are contained in unfamiliar words, and lead students to formulate definitions based upon the meanings of their parts. Finally, provide definitions for any words that remain undefined. **(Definitions of starred words are in the glossaries that follow the Vocabulary Lists. Definitions are *not* provided for the other words in the Vocabulary Lists.)**

Reread the list in random order and have students repeat each word after you. Then point to the words in random order and have the students pronounce each one without your assistance. Return to any words that students have difficulty pronouncing until they can pronounce them correctly. **This process will be repeated each day that students are working on a particular Discussion Guide, so if students still have difficulty pronouncing some of the words, they will have other opportunities for practice and correction**.

Next, lead students in completing the **Vocabulary Prediction Chart.** The importance of this activity lies in encouraging students to make logical connections between what they have been told about the reading selection and specific vocabulary words. **Being correct about predictions is not important; the thought process required to make predictions is**.

The graphic organizer should be put on chart paper so that the list can remain posted as students read the section of the reading selection in which the words first appear. Introduce words in subsequent Discussion Guides similarly.

Vocabulary List A

crimson (p. 5)
gazed (p. 5)
anxiously (p. 5)
jagged (p. 5)
weariness (p. 5)
captivity (p. 5)
tempest (p. 5)
clung (p. 5)
lashed (p. 6)
seething (p. 6)
brandishing (p. 6)
*oblivious (p. 6)
agonizing (adj., p. 7)
currents (p. 7)
copse (p. 7)
*makeshift (p. 7)
comrades (p. 8)
drenched (p. 8)
startled (p. 8)

lair (p. 8)
amphibian (p. 8)
unkempt (p. 8)
bedraggled (p. 8)
encrusted (p. 8)
radiantly (p. 8)
recounted (p. 9)
*ordeal (p. 9)
brine (p. 9)
tunic (p. 9)
astonished (adj., p. 9)
transformed (p. 9)
fascinated (p. 10)
ravenous (p. 10)
meadows (p. 10)
mosaics (p. 10)
arrayed (p. 10)
ornamental (p. 10)
*sumptuous (p. 10)

dominated (p. 10)
gracious (p. 11)
hospitality (p. 12)
apparent (p. 13)
sneered (p. 13)
insolent (p. 13)
momentum (p. 13)
arthritic (p. 14)
melancholy (adj., p. 14)
*distress (n., p. 14)
roused (p. 14)
dazzled (p. 14)
token (p. 14)
arrogant (p. 14)
plundered (p. 15)
stowed (p. 15)
vast (p. 15)
withered (p. 15)
plucked (p. 15)

Special Glossary

Adriatic Sea - the sea between northern Italy and Greece

Ithaca - a small island off the western coast of Greece

rudder - a flat piece of wood at the back of a boat, used for steering

mast - a tall pole on a boat used to hold the sail or sails

trident - a large, three-pronged fish spear used by Poseidon

nymph - a young, minor nature goddess associated with rivers and trees

inlet - a narrow bay

Athene - *variation of* Athena: the goddess of wisdom

Lebanon - a Middle Eastern country famous for magnificent cedar trees

Hades - (HAY-deez) the underworld or land of the dead, according to Greek mythology

discus - a heavy, flat disk of wood or metal, thrown for distance in competition

bard - a minstrel; a composer and singer of epic poetry

Olympian - associated with the Greek gods, who were said to live on Mt. Olympus

Trojan War - the long war in which the Greek kingdoms attacked the city of Troy

Achilles (Ah-KILL-eez)- Greek hero of the *Iliad*, who was killed in the Trojan War

Achaean (Uh-KAY-un) - having to do with the oldest Greek civilizations

lyre - a musical instrument, similar to a small harp

Glossary of Starred Words

oblivious - unaware

makeshift - put together in a hurry; do-it-yourself; improvised

ordeal - a very painful or challenging experience

sumptuous - rich; elegant; generous and fancy

distress - serious pain or unhappiness

Sample Meaningful Sentences for Starred Words

1. **Oblivious** to our promise to visit Grandma today, Dad agreed to go to the ball game, then had to cancel at the last minute.

2. Little Wendell's backyard hideout was a **makeshift** tent made of an old bedspread thrown over two lawn chairs.

3. After Isaac spent twelve painful, scary hours in the hospital, he said he never wanted to go through such an **ordeal** again.

4. For dinner, Grandma had prepared a **sumptuous** meal including roast turkey, potato salad, watermelon pickle, corn bread, and blackberry pie.

5. Alana was so upset that she locked herself in her room and refused to speak, so no one knew what to do to relieve her **distress**.

continued...

The Writer's Craft

Epic Poetry

An **epic** is a long narrative poem about the deeds of warriors and heroes. Epic poems bring together many elements on a grand scale: myths, legends, folk tales and history. The earliest epic poems, such as the *Odyssey*, began as traditional songs. They were passed on by word of mouth, often for many generations, before they were collected and written down. They are often important to a particular national culture because they express its highest ideals and its sense of its own origins and history.

The *Odyssey*, like other traditional epics, was originally written in poetry. Also, it was written in Greek. It included twelve sections or "books"! Today, several translations of the *Odyssey* in poetry are available in English. There are also shortened adaptations of the story written in prose (the ordinary language of speaking and writing), like this one.

Allusions

Since epics bring together a number of different stories, all connected in one way or another, we should not be surprised to find they are full of **allusions**. An allusion is a reference to a person or thing that is not really part of the story at this point. As you read the first section of the *Odyssey*, you will notice that the characters often refer to various Greek gods and heroes. Like political, sports, and entertainment heroes in our culture today, these mythical gods and heroes were familiar figures to the ancient Greeks. No one had to stop to explain to them that "fair Athene" was the goddess of wisdom – just as no one has to explain to you that Martin Luther King, Jr., was a civil rights hero, or that LeBron James plays basketball. Don't worry, though. These allusions are not too hard to understand, because in most cases, the author has included an explanation with each one.

DISCUSSION QUESTIONS AND ACTIVITIES

Section I. Read chapters 1-3 (pages 5-15). Discuss your responses to the questions and activities with a classmate. Then write your answers separately.

1. **The first chapter contains a number of hints and clues about Odysseus' past. What are some of these hints? What conclusions can we draw from them?** We learn from Chapter 1 that Odysseus had seen the Mediterranean dawn a thousand times before, and that he recognizes the rocks on the horizon as "Ithaca, his island home." The text mentions "seventeen sleepless days and nights alone at sea" and "twenty long years of war, wandering, and captivity." We can conclude that Odysseus is originally from Ithaca, but that he has been away from home for a long time and has recently undergone great suffering. He sees Poseidon, god of the sea, threatening him from within the storm, and the sea nymph Ino asks him what he has done to anger Poseidon. This suggests that some past offense to the sea god may be the reason for Odysseus' present suffering.

2. **Gods, goddesses, and other supernatural beings play an important part in Odysseus' story. What examples do we see in chapter 1? What does this suggest about the way the Greeks viewed the world?** In chapter 1, Odysseus is within sight of his homeland when Poseidon, the sea god, stirs up a storm that quickly overpowers his small boat and sweeps him back out to sea, leaving him half dead. Later, as Odysseus floats among the wreckage, a sea nymph intervenes with good advice and a magic scarf that will enable him to reach land again. This first chapter suggests that the Greeks saw themselves as being very much at the mercy of supernatural powers that could be cruel or kind at whim. However, they also recognized a significant measure of human responsibility. Ino assumes that Odysseus must have done something to make Poseidon so angry. Also, although Ino (EE-noh) helps Odysseus by giving him the magic scarf as a flotation device, he still must swim with the current in order to reach land.

3. **Nausicaa and her companions react very differently when they see Odysseus on the beach. Why does he seem so frightening to the companions? Why does Nausicaa find him attractive? What practical help does she offer him?** Nausicaa's companions are frightened because Odysseus is naked and unkempt, and

they take him for a wild animal or a woodland spirit. Nausicaa, however, stands her ground and listens to his story. She feels sorry for him when she hears about the shipwreck and sees the bruises on his body. She is also impressed by his gracious way of speaking, as well as the delicacy and good manners he shows in eating. Odysseus' situation both intrigues her and fills her with compassion; she concludes that he must be a man who is close to the gods, and she finds him distinctly attractive. She offers him a meal and some clothing, and takes him to the palace of her father, the king of the land.

4. **Why does Odysseus excuse himself from telling his story on his first day at King Alcinous'** (Al-KIN-oh-oos) **court? What event convinces the people of the court that Odysseus is in fact a very important and unusual person?** Odysseus excuses himself from telling his story for several reasons. He realizes that his listeners would be astonished to learn his real identity and might even doubt his word. Because of the shipwreck, he has no way to prove his claims. In addition, his story is a long one, and he is too tired to tell it all. King Alcinous graciously accepts Odysseus' refusal and offers him the finest hospitality anyway. However, the skepticism of certain courtiers becomes apparent at the athletic competition the next day when Euralyus (You-RAY-ley-us), the discus thrower, questions whether Odysseus is anyone special at all. Odysseus responds to this challenge by throwing a larger, heavier discus farther than anyone present has done previously, convincing his audience that he is indeed someone of great stature.

5. **When the bard Demodocus** (Deh-MOH-duck-us) **begins to sing, Odysseus is at first surprised and thrilled. Later, he is moved to tears. Explain these two emotional reactions. What does Odysseus ask Demodocus to sing about?** Odysseus is initially astonished that a man so apparently old and feeble as the aged, blind Demodocus would still sing so beautifully. Later, he begins to weep because Demodocus is singing about Odysseus' experience during the Trojan war, in particular his quarrel with Achilles, another Greek hero. This song stirs painful memories for Odysseus. His last request to Demodocus is for another song of the Trojan War, telling the story of the wooden horse that enabled the Greeks to finally win the war.

Make a
Prediction:

Will King Alcinous and his courtiers be surprised when they learn Odysseus' true identity?

Guided Discussion:

Discuss some of the key questions and activities in Section I. Also, feel free to ask questions not included in the Discussion Guide. Ask students to identify some of the allusions they may have noticed while reading this section. These include the following:

"Artemis (ART-eh-miss) the huntress, daughter of mighty Zeus" (page 8)

"three-headed Cerberus (SIR-burr-us), the dreadful dog that guards the gates of Hades" (page 10)

"Ares, son of great Zeus and god of war" (page 13)

"Aphrodite, goddess of love, and... [her] husband, Hephaestus (Heff-ESS-teez), god of fire and forge" (page 14)

Ask students what they notice about these allusions. They might point out that all of them have to do with Greek mythology, and that almost all refer to gods and goddesses. Point out that these allusions show us how completely the Greeks' religious belief system influenced their perception of the world around them.

 Vocabulary Prediction Check-up

Return to the vocabulary prediction chart, and use it to check the predictions students made prior to reading this section of the book. Remind students that, even if their predictions did not prove true, the value was in making them.

Vocabulary List B

siege (p. 16)
endured (p. 16)
morale (p. 16)
cunning (p. 16)
dismantled (p. 16)
nerve-racking (p. 17)
sentinels (p. 17)
stupor (p. 17)
slaughter (p. 17)
ransacked (p. 18)
venerable (p. 18)
perished (p. 18)
intense (p. 19)
barrage (p. 19)
draught p. 19)
sectors (p. 20)
exultant (p. 20)
stifling (p. 20)

disembarked (p. 20)
piracy (p. 20)
orgy (p. 20)
*replenish (p. 20)
diminishing (p. 20)
pillaged (p. 20)
*complacent (p. 20)
overwhelmed (p. 21)
*exuberant (p. 21)
foreboding (p. 21)
*despondent (p. 22)
savoring (p. 22)
luxuriant (p. 22)
vegetation (p. 22)
moored (p. 23)
clambered (p. 23)
outraged (p. 23)
colossus (p. 23)

boulder (p. 23)
rekindled (p. 23)
cowered (p. 23)
suppliants (p. 24)
bulbous (p. 24)
gruesome (p. 24)
consumed (p. 24)
scheme (n., p. 24)
brutality (p. 25)
heady (p. 25)
irresistible (p. 25)
undiluted (p. 26)
slackened (p. 26)
embers (p. 26)
clamored (p. 28)
*dissuade (p. 28)
sacrifice (n., p. 29)

Special Glossary

Sparta - one of the Greek kingdoms, located on the Peloponnese (*below*)

Peloponnese - the large peninsula that made up the southern portion of Greece (a canal was dug that separated it from the mainland and made it an island in 1893)

gale-force wind - a very strong wind (over 32 miles per hour)

Cythera - (*var. of* Kíthira) a small island just south of Peloponnese

Libya - a country in central North Africa, across the Mediterranean Sea from Greece

laurel - an evergreen shrub with large, shiny leaves

whey - the liquid left over when milk is made into cheese

rams, billy goats - male sheep and goats

ewes, milking goats - female sheep and goats

Apollo - god of the sun in Greek mythology

fleeces - coats of wool (of sheep and similar animals)

prow - the front of a boat or ship

Glossary of Starred Words

replenish -to refill; to stock up

complacent - self-satisfied; smug; not worrying about anything

exuberant - in high spirits; joyful; wildly excited

despondent - despairing; hopeless; very discouraged

dissuade - to persuade *not* to do something; to advise against

Sample Meaningful Sentences for Starred Words

1. I must **replenish** my stock of pencils for school, since I have used up or lost most of the ones I had at the beginning of the year.

2. After five straight wins the players became **complacent** and lazy, so yesterday they lost to a team they should have beaten easily.

3. When school was dismissed early because of snow, the children were so **exuberant** with joy that the bus driver stopped to wait until they calmed down.

4. My sister was so **despondent** when her boyfriend broke up with her that she hardly ate anything for three days.

5. When Deeondra's friends told her they were going to cut class, she tried to **dissuade** them because she knew they would be in big trouble.

The Writer's Craft

Story-Within-A-Story

A **story-within-a-story** is just what it sounds like: a character in the story you are reading begins to tell another story. It could be a story from the character's imagination, or it could be a story of something that happened in the past. Sometimes a writer will set off the story-within-a-story in quotation marks, or will use italics to set it apart from the main story. In other cases, however, the writer gives no punctuation clues, and we must read carefully to determine where the story-within-a-story ends and the main story picks up again.

Chapter 4 begins with Demodocus' story about the wooden horse and the Trojan War. Can you tell where Demodocus' story ends? How do you know?

"In medias res"

This Latin phrase means "into the middle of things." The **in medias res** technique consists of starting the story somewhere in the middle, usually at an exciting point. For example, this version of the *Odyssey* began with Odysseus, in sight of his island home, being blown off course and shipwrecked. However, as we will soon discover, this is not the beginning of the story – in fact, this event is somewhere near the end! Starting in Chapter 5, Odysseus goes back to tell the story, from the beginning, for his hosts in King Alcinous' court. Read carefully to make sure you understand the order in which the events recounted actually occurred.

Homer's epic poems, the *Iliad* and the *Odyssey*, are among the oldest known examples in the world of this literary technique. However, it is still very popular today. For instance, you will often find it in the "drama in real life" stories in popular magazines. The article begins with the main character in some exciting, challenging, or dangerous situation. Then the writer goes back to tell us how the character came to be in that situation. Finally, the story goes on to tell us how the character resolves the problem or escapes the danger. Watch for examples in magazines, television shows, and movies!

DISCUSSION QUESTIONS AND ACTIVITIES

Section II. Read chapters 4-5 (pages 16-29). Discuss answers to the following questions with a classmate, then write your answers separately.

1. **The story of the wooden horse contains hints of both the strong points and the weak points that we will observe over and over again in Odysseus' character. In the T-chart below, list some of the strengths and weaknesses you observe in Odysseus' character in this account. Give an example of each quality that you list. Why do you think Odysseus weeps uncontrollably when Demodocus finishes his song?** Possible answers for the T-chart are as follows.

Odysseus' Strengths	Odysseus' Weaknesses
cunning (thinks up the plan of the wooden horse)	pride (like others, he pursued the war mainly for pride's sake)
patience (waiting in the wooden horse)	cruelty (wholesale slaughter of Troy)
courage (leads the attack on the palace)	lack of leadership (fails to control his men in their excesses)

Odysseus probably weeps at the end of Demodocus' song, partly in sorrow for the comrades he has lost, and partly in regret for failing to prevent the atrocities his men committed at Troy.

2. **How does Odysseus describe the state of mind of his men as they finally left Troy? What happened to change their mood?** According to Odysseus, his men were in high spirits when they finally left Troy. They had won their war and filled their ships with riches taken from the conquered city. Even though they were blown northward instead of south, they took advantage of the circumstance by pillaging Ismarus (ISS-mar-us), the town where they docked. Unfortunately, in their relish they became careless. They spent the night on shore, drinking and carousing. At dawn, the townspeople returned with reinforcements and drove them away, killing several men from each ship. This spoiled their good mood and made them realize that their journey was still far from over.

3. **What do you think of Odysseus' men, based on the description of their behavior in Ismarus and Libya? What do you think of Odysseus' leadership in these situations?** The behavior of

Odysseus' men in Ismarus and Libya deserves no respect. Although the negative effects of ten years at war may be adduced to partially excuse them, their rampage through a town with which they had no quarrel is shocking. Odysseus excuses their behavior, saying, "...after four days at sea, it was sensible to replenish our diminishing stores of food and wine." However, the men plunder and slaughter innocent people for sheer pleasure. Their decision to spend the night carousing on the shore indicates a lack of prudence and foresight. The ease with which they succumb to the temptations of the lotus fruit also shows their weakness of character. As for Odysseus' leadership, we notice that he fails to convince his men to leave Ismarus in a timely manner, instead deciding to participate in their raucous, imprudent celebration. (We do learn later that he managed to protect the priest of Apollo and his family from the Greeks' brutality.) When his men get in trouble with the lotus-eaters, however, he takes charge, binding them with ropes and forcing them to return to the ship.

4. **Odysseus plans a very clever escape from the Cyclops'** (SIE-klops) **cave, thinking ahead about ways to avoid the many risks involved. In one column of the chart below, list the different tricks Odysseus thinks of to defeat the Cyclops. In the other column, tell how each trick contributes to the men's safety and successful escape.** Possible answers are shown.

Odysseus' Tricks	How the Tricks Helped the Men Escape
He told the Cyclops that he and the 12 men with him were the only survivors from a shipwreck.	He did not want the Cyclops to go looking for the rest of the fleet and catch them as well.
He cut a pole from a tree trunk and sharpened its end to a point.	He had to blind the Cyclops, so the Cyclops would not see the men escaping.
He gave the Cyclops special, very strong wine to drink.	He wanted the Cyclops to be drunk so that he and his men could get into position to blind him with the sharpened pole.
He told the Cyclops that his name was Noman.	When the Cyclops began to yell for help, he told the other Cyclopes that "Noman" had attacked him. The others thought he meant that "no man" was there, so they didn't come to help him.
He fastened his men and himself to the bellies of the rams that were about to go out to pasture.	The Cyclops felt the backs of the animals to see if anyone was escaping, but he didn't feel under their bellies, so the men got away.

5. **Odysseus makes one terrible mistake in the escape from the Cyclops. Why does he insist on telling the Cyclops his real name after his ship leaves the shore? Why is this a mistake?** Odysseus' pride is the fatal flaw that leads him to tell the Cyclops his real name as he is escaping. This is a mistake because once the Cyclops knows his real name, he can put a terrible curse on him, calling down the wrath of his father, the sea god Poseidon, on Odysseus and his men.

6. **Think back to the beginning of the book. Explain why this incident (the escape from the Cyclops) is so important for understanding the rest of Odysseus' adventures.** The escape from the Cyclops is important because we remember that it is Poseidon who drives Odysseus away from Ithaca when he is within sight of it in Chapter 1, and we realize that his wrath is a fulfillment of the Cyclops' curse. We also notice the second part of the curse: "however, if he's fated to return, make sure that his journey's long and miserable, that all his companions die, and that his is a bitter homecoming." We can guess that the rest of the story will tell us how this curse is fulfilled. The incident with the Cyclops is significant because it is the departure point, as well as the explanation, for all of Odysseus' subsequent wanderings and sufferings.

Make a
Prediction:

What dangers will Odysseus and his men encounter after they leave the small island?

Guided Discussion:

Discuss some of the key questions and activities in Section II. In addition, feel free to include in your discussion questions that are not in the Discussion Guide. You may want to make a horizontal or vertical timeline, as follows.

20 years previous ● Beginning of the Trojan War

10 years after that ● End of the Trojan War/ wooden horse incident
(also 10 years
before shipwreck) ● Attack on Ismarus

● Encounter with the lotus-eaters

● Adventure with the Cyclops

(10 years go by...)

?

time when story is ● Shipwreck near Ithaca
being told ● Visit to Alcinous' court at Phaeicia

Point out to students the *large empty space* between the events recounted in Chapters 5-6 (the events surrounding and immediately following the fall of Troy), and Odysseus' shipwreck and visit to Alcinous' court. Tell students that the next section of the story will fill in the gaps, recounting the events that occurred during this period of time that is still a blank as far as we are concerned.

 ## Vocabulary Prediction Check-up

Return to the vocabulary prediction chart, and use it to check the predictions students made prior to reading this section of the book. Remind students that, even if their predictions did not prove true, the value was in making them.

Selection Review

1. **Who is Odysseus? What do we learn from these chapters about his past?** Odysseus, the king of the small Greek island of Ithaca, is also a military leader and hero. We learn that he left his home twenty years earlier to lead troops in the Greeks' war against the city of Troy. The war went on for ten years before the Greeks finally won. However, Odysseus did not succeed in returning to his home when the war was over. He has been wandering around the Mediterranean Sea for the past ten years. He has suffered a great deal during that time.

2. **How does Odysseus arrive at King Alcinous' court? What makes King Alcinous and his nobles realize that Odysseus is an unusual and important person?** Odysseus was drawing near Ithaca, his island home, when a terrible storm tipped his boat over. Odysseus was thrown into the water. He had to swim for his life. He finally washed up on the shore of Phaeicia. Nausicaa, the daughter of the king of Phaeicia, gave him food and clothing and took him to her father's court. King Alcinous and his nobles realized that Odysseus was an unusual and important person when he threw the discus farther than their champion athletes. They also noticed him weeping as he listened to their court singer telling the stories of the Trojan War, so they guessed that he had something to do with that war.

3. **What are some of the good qualities that made Odysseus such a hero to the Greeks? Give some examples from the text.** First, Odysseus is a clever, intelligent leader. For example, he thought up the trick with the wooden horse that helped the Greeks win the Trojan War. He also thought up a clever plan to trick the Cyclops when he and his men were trapped in the giant's cave. Second, Odysseus is very brave. He led his men in the attack on Troy. He also led the plan to blind the Cyclops and escape from him. Finally, Odysseus is patient. He waited patiently in the wooden horse until night when he and his men could come out. He has been trying to reach home for ten years, but he still has not given up hope.

4. **What are some of Odysseus' weak points? What are some of the consequences he has suffered because of his mistakes?** One of Odysseus' weak points is that he does not exercise leadership to make his men do what is right. Instead, he often goes along with them, even when he knows that what they are doing is wrong. For example, he took part in the terrible killing at Troy.

The Greeks killed old people, women, and children as well as soldiers. Afterward, they attacked Ismarus for no reason at all. They again killed innocent people and looted their goods. Odysseus knew this was wrong, but he did not stop his men. Then, he knew they should leave before the townspeople came back. Instead, he let his men talk him into staying on the beach and partying all night. They were attacked at dawn and several men were killed. Odysseus' greatest fault, however, is his pride. His pride leads him to tell the Cyclops his real name as he escapes. The Cyclops curses him, calling on the sea god Poseidon to ruin his trip and keep him from reaching home safely. This curse leads to all of Odysseus' later troubles.

5. **What do we learn from this text about the Greeks' view of the gods? What role do gods, goddesses, and other supernatural beings play in Odysseus' adventures?** We see in the text that the gods and goddesses were very important in the Greeks' view of life. They believed that the gods could be jealous or moody, and that they acted directly in people's affairs. For example, when Odysseus senses danger, he asks the goddess Athena to help him. All his troubles occur because the god Poseidon is angry with him. When he is shipwrecked, he survives because a sea nymph, Ino, gives him good advice, as well as a magic scarf to help him swim to shore.

Informational Text Connections

Types of informational text with connections to these chapters include:

    Illustrated juvenile non-fiction texts on ancient Greece
    Age-appropriate encyclopedia or other articles on the ancient Greek pantheon
    Maps of Greece and the Mediterranean world, showing both ancient and modern place names

Select a text appropriate to your students' reading level and interests. Have them read and analyze the text using applicable criteria from the Common Core Standards. (Remember that different texts will lend themselves to different approaches for comprehension and analysis.)

Literature-Related Writing

1. Write a true account of an exciting event in your life or the life of someone you know. Use the ***in medias res*** technique.

2. Pretend you are a reporter for the *Ithaca Inquirer*. Write a **news report** of the Greeks' victory in the city of Troy.

3. Pretend you were one of the men in Odysseus' ship. Write at least three **journal entries** telling about your adventures, from the end of the war against Troy up to the escape from the island of the Cyclops

 Extension Activities

1. Research the events that were supposed to have occurred during the Trojan War, which form the background for the *Odyssey*. Report what you learn to your class.

2. Research the Greek gods and goddesses. Create a poster or chart to show what you learn.

3. Draw a picture or create a model to illustrate an episode in the story.

Literature Test

1. **Who is Odysseus? How does he come to be at King Alcinous' court in Phaeicia?** Odysseus is the king of the Greek island of Ithaca. He left his home twenty years earlier to fight in the Trojan War, which lasted ten years. After that, he struggled unsuccessfully for ten more years to return home. When he finally came within sight of his home, the sea god, Poseidon, shipwrecked his boat and sent him back out to sea, where he washed up on the shore of Phaeicia. Nausicaa, King Alcinous' daughter, found him and took him to her father's court.

2. **One of Odysseus' strong points was his cleverness. Tell how Odysseus' cleverness helped him, both in ending the Trojan War and in escaping from the Cyclops.** Odysseus showed his cleverness when he planned the building of a huge wooden horse with soldiers hidden inside it so they could get into the city of Troy to destroy it. Later, when the Cyclops trapped him

and his men, Odysseus came up with a complicated plan to escape. He blinded the Cyclops. Then he tied his men to the rams' bellies so that they could leave the cave without the giant realizing they were doing so.

3. **List two of Odysseus' weaknesses as a leader. Explain how each of these weaknesses caused trouble for Odysseus and his men.** One of Odysseus' weaknesses was that he did not make his men do the right thing. Because he allowed them to kill and plunder innocent people, then to spend the night partying, several of his men were killed at Ismarus. Odysseus' other great weakness was his pride. In his pride, he insisted on telling the Cyclops his real name as he and his men escaped. This information enabled the Cyclops to curse Odysseus and his men, calling down the anger of the great sea god, Poseidon, on them.

4. **How are the gods and goddesses involved in Odysseus' life? Give at least two specific examples.** Gods and goddesses play an important role in Odysseus' life. He calls on the goddess of wisdom, Athena, to help him when he is in trouble. The curse of the sea god, Poseidon, is the source of most of his troubles. A sea nymph, Ino, rescues him when his boat is shipwrecked. (Students should cite any two of these examples.)

Discussion Guide #2

Chapters 6 - 10 (pages 30-61)

Vocabulary List A

desolate (p. 30)
*subdued (adj., p. 30)
extraordinary (p. 30)
encasing (p. 30)
trepidation (p. 30)
checkered (p. 30)
vigilance (p. 30)
*anticipation (p. 30)
folly (p. 31)
hurling (p. 31)
unpredictable (p. 31)
provisions (p. 31)
brooded (p. 32)
meandered (p. 32)

sinuous (p. 32)
carcass (p. 33)
vantage point (p. 33)
reluctance (p. 33)
*alternative (n., p. 33)
enchanted (adj., p. 33)
inexpressibly (p. 33)
enticingly (p. 33)
intricate (p. 35)
stupefying (p. 35)
*sensation (p. 35)
imploringly (p. 36)
vile (p. 36)

resigned (adj., p. 38)
dismayed (adj., p. 38)
perpetual (p. 39)
dwindled (p. 39)
blighted (adj., p. 39)
*recognition (p. 40)
pierced (p. 40)
perilous (p. 40)
pining (p. 41)
*treacherous (p. 42)
deceived (p. 43)
agony (p. 43)
din (p. 43)

Special Glossary

four winds - The Greeks imagined four winds (north, south, east, and west) as four personal beings. Winds are named for the direction they come from; thus, a west wind blows a ship toward the east.

crag - a steep, rugged rock that rises above the surrounding area

stag - a male deer

venison - deer meat

sties - enclosures or pens for pigs

swine - pigs

timbers - the mast and spars (vertical and horizontal poles) of a ship

rigging - the network of ropes holding a ship's sails in place

hold - the bottom of a ship, the part used to hold cargo

river Ocean - in the Greek view, Ocean was a river flowing all around the world's edge

Thrinacia - (Thrin-AY-shuh) usually identified as modern-day Sicily

pretenders - people who claim that they should be king or ruler of a country

Glossary of Starred Words

subdued - quiet; downhearted; discouraged

anticipation - eagerness; the act of looking forward to something

alternative - a different choice or possibility

sensation - a feeling

recognition - awareness; the act of recognizing

treacherous - deceitful; disloyal; tricky

Sample Meaningful Sentences for Starred Words

1. When Grandma went to the hospital, the children were quiet and **subdued**, wondering whether she would ever be the same again.

2. We put up a large "Welcome Home" sign in **anticipation**, happy that Momma was coming back after two weeks away.

3. Trevor decided to attend summer school since it was the only **alternative** to repeating the course the following school year.

4. Mandy turned around slowly because she had a strange **sensation** oft someone staring at her from behind.

5. I didn't expect to know anyone at the citywide band clinic, so my eyes lit up in **recognition** when I saw a girl I knew from elementary school.

6. We learned that some **treacherous** kids from our block were spying on our practices, then selling information on our plays to the team from Dumfries Park.

 ## The Writer's Craft

Personification and *Anthropomorphism*

Personification is a figure of speech in which an inanimate object or idea is compared to a human being. For instance, we might describe it as having feelings or desires, or as doing something that only people actually do. We use this in everyday speech—for example, when we say, "This cold just *doesn't want to give up*," or, "I can't find my new CD; I guess it must have *gone for a walk*."

However, sometimes in literature personification is taken to a different level. Non-human creatures and things may be treated as if they actually *are* people or personal beings. This is called **anthropomorphism**. It is particularly common in mythology. The Greeks really believed that various types of spirits, nymphs, and gods ruled things in nature, such as rivers, trees, and oceans. In the next section, we read about three of the four winds (north, south, east, and west) being shut up in a bag. The Greeks could imagine shutting up the winds in a bag because they imagined them as personal beings who would blow differently depending on the mood they were in (for example, angry, playful, or peaceful).

Symbolism

A **symbol** is a visible object that represents an invisible reality or idea. One symbol widely recognized today is the bald eagle as a symbol of the United States. The ancient world also had well-known symbols, many of them linked to religious practices and traditions. In the next section, Odysseus sacrifices sheep before he is allowed to enter the world of the dead. What do you think the blood of the sacrifice might symbolize to ancient people?

DISCUSSION QUESTIONS AND ACTIVITIES

Section I. Read chapters 6-7 (pages 30-43). Discuss answers to the following questions with a classmate, then write your answers separately.

1. **Odysseus hoped that Aeolus'** (Ay-OH-luss) **gift would enable him to reach home safely. Why? What happens instead?** Aeolus' gift to Odysseus is to confine three of the four winds in a bag, which Odysseus is not to open until the remaining fourth wind has blown his ship to Ithaca. Odysseus guards the bag carefully until he and his fleet are within sight of Ithaca. Then, relieved, he falls into a deep sleep. While he sleeps, his men, apparently unaware of the bag's contents, open it up to share the treasure. As soon as the three imprisoned winds are set free, they blow up a terrible storm that drives the fleet back out to sea.

2. **What human faults or mistakes contribute to this failure? What conclusion does Aeolus draw when he hears their story?** Odysseus' failure to remain vigilant right to the end, and his men's impatience and greed, are the human factors contributing to this disaster. However, when Aeolus hears what happened to them, he concludes (with typical Greek fatalism) that the gods oppose Odysseus and his men, and he refuses to help them further.

3. **Think about Odysseus' adventures with the Laestrogonians** (LIE-struh-GO-nee-uns, **pages 31-32)** and with Circe (SIR-see, **pages 32-28). Some aspects of these two stories are very similar, while others are very different. Using the Venn diagram below, compare and contrast the two stories.** Some possible answers are shown.

Adventure with the Laestrogonians

a city on a hill

Cruel giants tear the men apart and start to devour them openly.

Odysseus feels lucky to escape with his life and his ship.

no help from the gods

The survivors leave as fast as they can.

Both

Those who stay behind are saved, but those who go ahead meet with disaster.

Things are not as they seem: an apparent welcome is really a trick.

Spies come back to tell Odysseus what has happened

Adventure with Circe

a quiet natural harbor

A woman with the voice of a goddess welcomes the men, gives them food and drink that put them to sleep, then turns them into animals.

Odysseus vows to avenge his men.

Hermes (HER-meez) offers helps.

Odysseus makes Circe free the men, then they stay there for another year.

4. **Imagine you were one of Odysseus' men. Would you have wanted to accept Circe's invitation to stay in her palace? Why or why not?** Answers may vary. Some students may agree with Odysseus' men, saying that after all the hardships of the voyage up to this point, they deserve a break, courtesy of the lovely Circe and her maids. Others may point out that Odysseus and his men still know practically nothing about Circe, and the little they know is not likely to inspire confidence. Even though she may be bound by her oath not to harm them, she may have other, more insidious forms of enchantment; at the least, time spent with Circe and her maids is time lost as far as returning to their homes and families is concerned. In addition, this invitation to casual sex and, for many, adultery, presents a significant moral choice – one to which, unfortunately, Odysseus and his men seem utterly indifferent.

5. **Describe Odysseus' feelings as he travels to the land of the dead. Why do you think the ghosts crowd forward toward the blood of the sheep Odysseus has sacrificed? (What does the blood symbolize, and how does drinking it affect them?)** Odysseus feels sick with fear as he travels to the land of the dead, since no living person has ever gone to Hades and returned alive. The ghosts crowd forward at the smell of the sacrificed animals' blood because they want to drink it. The blood symbolizes life; when the ghosts drink it, they are able to recognize the living and converse with them, at least for a short time.

6. **Odysseus learns useful information from his conversations with the dead. In one case, he is also able to provide useful information. Using the chart below, summarize the information that Odysseus exchanges with Tiresias** (Tie-REE-see-us)**, Anti-cleia** (An-tick-LAY-uh, **Odysseus' mother**)**, Agamemnon** (Ag-uh-MEM-non)**, and Achilles.** Some possible answers are shown.

Identity of Ghost	What Odysseus Learns From Him/Her	What Odysseus Tells Him/Her
Tiresias, a prophet	Poseidon is still out to get Odysseus. He must avoid the island of Thrinacia; if any of his men harm the herds of the sun god, they will be doomed. If Odysseus reaches home, he will find unwelcome guests trying to take his wife and throne.	(n/a)
Anticleia, Odysseus' mother	Odysseus' father, wife and son are still alive. Penelope has remained faithful, despite pressure; Telemachus is a fine young man.	(n/a)
Agamemnon, commander of the Greek army at Troy	Agamemnon was betrayed by his wife and killed as soon as he arrived home.	(n/a)
Achilles, finest of the Greek warriors	Achilles would rather be the poorest man alive than a prince among the dead.	Achilles' son has grown into a wise, brave warrior and has become wealthy from the riches of Troy.

Make a
Prediction:

What dangers await Odysseus and his men after they leave the land of the dead?

Guided Discussion:

Discuss some of the key questions and activities in Section I. In addition, feel free to include in your discussion questions that are not in the Discussion Guide. You might want to ask students to compare Odysseus' and Penelope's behavior during their long years of separation. Penelope, of course, is praised for her faithfulness; Odysseus is not faithful, and the narrative seems to present his unfaithfulness as excusable, almost justifiable. Ask students what this double standard suggests about the ancient Greek view of men and women, their roles and relationships. Invite students to comment on this and to give reasons for their views.

 Vocabulary Prediction Check-up

Return to the vocabulary prediction chart, and use it to check the predictions students made prior to reading this section of the book. Remind students that, even if their predictions did not prove true, the value was in making them.

Vocabulary List B

murky (p. 44)	menacingly (p. 47)	yearned (p. 55)
prospect (n., p. 44)	ghastly (p. 48)	flinched (p. 55)
*unscathed (p. 45)	tempo (p. 50)	entranced (p. 56)
vengeful (p. 45)	*impending (p. 50)	threshold (p. 57)
navigation (p. 45)	grueling (p. 50)	massive (p. 57)
turbulent (p. 45)	*exertions (p. 51)	burnished (p. 57)
chaos (p. 45)	scoured (p. 51)	soothing (p. 60)
wallows (v., p. 46)	tether (n., p. 51)	idle (adj., p. 60)
tentacles (p. 46)	summit (p. 52)	mortals (p. 61)
recesses (p. 46)	breach (n., p. 52)	pursued (p. 61)
prey (n., p. 46)	writhe (p. 52)	cloak (p. 61)
contortions (p. 47)	abated (p. 53)	tattered (p. 61)
skirt (v., p. 47)	bulbous (p. 53)	
lurked (p. 47)	*regained (p. 54)	

Special Glossary

straits - narrow waterway connecting two larger bodies of water

headland - a point of land reaching out into the water

mainland - in this case, the mainland of Italy; the straits of Scylla (SKILL-uh) and Charybdis (Kuh-RIB-diss) are generally identified as the narrow passageway between Italy and Sicily

the elements - wind, rain, and the forces of nature that make up the weather

cove - a small, protected natural bay

game - wild animals hunted for food

adz - a sharp tool for trimming and smoothing wood

braces - (*boating*) ropes for moving the sails around

halyards - (*boating*) ropes for raising and lowering the sails

Great Bear - a constellation of stars in the northern sky; the Big Dipper is part of this constellation

locusts - insects similar to grasshoppers, known for greedily eating every green bit of plant they can find

swineherd - a farm worker who cares for pigs

Glossary of Starred Words

unscathed - unharmed

impending - coming; about to happen

exertions - efforts; hard work

regained - recovered; got back

Sample Meaningful Sentences for Starred Words

1. Darren was in a serious auto accident yesterday, but by a miracle, he walked away **unscathed**, without a scratch on him.

2. At the end of the semester the students were very nervous about the **impending** state math exam they would soon have to take.

3. We had worked very hard cleaning out Grandpa's shed, so when we finished, he thanked us for our **exertions** with a big pitcher of lemonade and a pizza.

4. Aunt Tina lost weight during her illness, but she quickly **regained** it when she felt better, and soon she was back to her usual shape.

The Writer's Craft

Complications

Complications are new difficulties or challenges that arise when things finally seem to be working out well. We have already seen many examples of complications as Odysseus has struggled to return to his home; every time he escapes one danger, he encounters another. Will the complications stop if he finally reach Ithaca? What do you think?

Irony

Irony is a term used to describe a situation in which what really happens is the opposite of what might have been expected. Ironies can be good or bad. For example, it is bitterly *ironic* that Odysseus' men let the winds loose when they were already within sight of their home (a bad irony). It is *ironic* that Circe, who once turned them into pigs, later turns out to be one of Odysseus' most trusted and helpful advisors (a good irony). Watch for more ironies, both good and bad, in the next section of the story!

DISCUSSION QUESTIONS AND ACTIVITIES

Section II. Read chapters 8-10 (pages 44-61). Discuss answers to the following questions with a classmate, then write your answers separately.

1. **When Odysseus and his men return to Circe's land, she takes Odysseus aside to advise him on the dangers he must face next.** *Summarize* **the warnings and advice that Circe gives Odysseus.** Circe tells Odysseus that the journey coming up is the most dangerous he has ever taken. First, he must block his ears against the deadly song of the Sirens, seemingly beautiful women who lure men to their death. Then, he must not sail around the western side of Thrinacia, where treacherous moving rocks would crush his ship. Instead, he must pass through the narrow straits where the monsters Scylla and Charybdis live. He must be careful to avoid Charybdis' whirlpool, and should expect Scylla to eat at least six of his men as they pass through. Finally, he and his men must not touch the herds of the sun god pastured on Thrinacia, for this would seal their doom.

2. **How do Odysseus and his men come through the dangers of the Sirens, Charybdis, and Scylla? Why do they return to Thrinacia, despite the warnings they have received to stay away from it?** Odysseus avoids the danger of the Sirens by plugging his men's ears with wax and having himself tied to a mast before he comes in hearing of the Sirens' enchanting song. The sailors escape Charybdis by rowing quickly to avoid her whirlpool, but, sadly, they cannot avoid danger completely; Scylla devours six of them as Circe had foretold. Unfortunately, after they come through all these dangers, they face a strong wind that blows them backward, in the direction opposite to the one they want. They finally give up fighting the wind and return to Thrinacia. After they land there, a violent storm blows up, and for weeks afterward, the wind is blowing in the wrong direction for them to continue their voyage. (**Note to teachers**: Have students find the strait between Italy and Sicily/Thrinacia on a map.)

3. **Why do Odysseus' men help themselves to the sun god's cattle, even though they know that this crime will be punished by death? Why is this *ironic*? How does this event fulfill the prophecies and warnings made earlier in the story?** Odysseus' men slaughter the sun god's cattle because their supplies are gone and they cannot find anything else to eat. They rationalize that if they do not kill the cattle, they will starve and perish anyway. They feel they have nothing to lose. They take advantage of Odysseus' absence from camp to kill the cattle, making sacrifices to the gods in an attempt to stave off the judgment they should incur. Ironically, they give in to temptation just hours before the wind changes, allowing them to leave Thrinacia. Of course, the judgment falls. As soon as they set out to sea, mighty Zeus himself blasts their ship with a thunderbolt, killing all but Odysseus. This fulfills the warnings given by Circe and Tiresias: "If any of your men lays a finger on these animals, then Zeus will destroy your ship and your crew." In addition, it fulfills the curse of the Cyclops: "... if he's fated to return, make sure that his journey's long and miserable [and] that all his companions die." After Zeus's judgment falls, all of Odysseus' companions are dead.

4. **What happens to Odysseus after the ship explodes? What is the problem with being rescued by Calypso** (Kuh-LIP-soh)**?** After Odysseus' ship explodes, he clings to the mast and floats with the current. He narrowly escapes destruction in the straits of Scylla and Charybdis and slowly floats westward. After nine days at sea he washes up on an island, where a sea nymph,

Calypso, finds him and nurses him back to health. Unfortunately, Calypso falls in love with him and refuses to let him leave for seven years. She offers him eternal life if he will agree to stay with her. Although she is very beautiful and her home is a paradise, Odysseus is unhappy; he longs to return to his own home and to his wife and son.

5. **Odysseus' story-within-a-story ends in Chapter 10, which finds him back in the court of King Alcinous. How does Alcinous help Odysseus? Notice what Alcinous says about his family background (page 56). Why is it ironic that he is the one who helps Odysseus reach his home at last?** Alcinous helps Odysseus by assigning a ship and crew to take him safely to Ithaca. It is ironic that Alcinous, who is himself a grandson of the sea god Poseidon, is the one who finally enables Odysseus to reach home in spite of Poseidon's curse on him.

6. **Why does Athene finally appear to Odysseus only after his arrival at Ithaca?** Athene finally comes to Odysseus after his arrival at Ithaca because this marks the end of Poseidon's curse on him, and the order of Zeus preventing the other gods and goddesses from interfering. She is, therefore, now at liberty to help him, and indeed he will need her help.

7. **What news does Athene bring Odysseus of his home? How does she offer to help him?** Athene confirms what others have already intimated: for four years: suitors, anxious to usurp Odysseus' throne, have besieged his wife and have been feasting on his wealth. They have even plotted to kill his son. Athene offers to disguise Odysseus as an old beggar. She advises him to stay with Eumaeus, a loyal swineherd, while she goes to fetch his son, Telemachus, who can help him deal with the unwelcome guests.

Make a
Prediction:

How will Odysseus get rid of the men who are trying to take his wife and his throne?

Guided Discussion:

Discuss some of the key questions and activities in Section II. In addition, feel free to include in your discussion questions that are not in the Discussion Guide. Ask students what **complications** Odysseus encounters in this section. Complications include being blown back to Thrinacia and stranded there, his men's decision to steal Hyperion's cattle despite their oath, Calypso's insistence that he stay with her, and, finally, the news that his home is crawling with would-be usurpers.

Ask students to describe Odysseus' response to Calypso's affections, and compare it to his earlier relationship with Circe. Although Odysseus appreciates Calypso's help and admires her beauty, he does not want to live with her, even when offered the possibility of immortality. He wants to return to his wife and his home. His unwillingness to stay with Calypso is in marked contrast to his behavior toward Circe, whose hospitality he cheerfully enjoyed until one of his men suggested that it was time to leave. Ask students why they think Odysseus' attitude is different this time. Answers may vary, as this is a speculative question. Perhaps Odysseus' sufferings have given him a new appreciation of his home and his marriage. Perhaps the reports that he has since heard of Penelope's faithfulness, despite very challenging circumstances, have inspired in him a desire to be worthy of her love and loyalty. Perhaps he is simply older and wiser. Perhaps losing all of his companions has awakened in him the desire to return to his remaining loved ones.

Although some of Odysseus' woes can be attributed to his errors and those of his men, other causes are completely beyond human control (and, in the Greek view, would be attributed to the intervention of the gods). Ask students to identify these events that are outside of human control. The most obvious is the strong southeasterly wind that drove the ship back to Thrinacia after it had escaped the perils of Scylla and Charybdis, then forced the men to remain there until they had eaten all of their provisions. Lead students in a discussion of the Greek view of human responsibility and the role of fate.

Vocabulary Prediction Check-up

Return to the vocabulary prediction chart, and use it to check the predictions students made prior to reading this section of the book. Remind students that, even if their predictions did not prove true, the value was in making them.

 Selection Review

1. **Aeolus tries to help Odysseus reach home. What goes wrong? What happens to most of Odysseus' ships and men?** Aeolus ties three of the winds in a bag, so that only the west wind is free to blow the fleet to Ithaca. He tells Odysseus to make sure the bag remains closed until they reach home. Unfortunately, Odysseus falls asleep once they are in sight of Ithaca. His men open the bag, and the other winds blow up a storm, driving the fleet back to Aeolus' island. Aeolus refuses to help them again. The fleet drifts around until it reaches a harbor. The giants who live there crush the ships and eat their crews. Only Odysseus' ship and its crew escape disaster.

2. **How does Circe trick the men? What changes this situation? What is ironic about what happens next?** Circe puts drugs in the drinks she offers Odysseus' men. Then she changes them into pigs. When Odysseus hears about this, he wants to rescue his men. The god Hermes gives him a plant to help him resist Circe's magic. Odysseus forces her to change his men back. Ironically, once Circe stops putting spells on the men, she offers them a warm welcome. She offers to make love to Odysseus. He agrees, and the men stay in her palace for about a year.

3. **Why does Odysseus sacrifice sheep when he visits the land of the dead? What useful information does he learn from the ghosts?** Odysseus sacrifices sheep so the ghosts can drink their blood. The warm blood gives the ghosts enough life to see Odysseus and talk with him for a short time. One of the ghosts, Tiresias, is an old prophet. He warns Odysseus about the dangers of his journey. He especially warns against killing any of the sun god's cattle. He tells Odysseus that unwanted guests in his palace want to become king in his place. Another ghost is Odysseus' mother. She tells him that his father, his wife, and his son are still alive. His wife still waits for him faithfully, but she is having trouble with unwanted guests.

4. **What does Circe tell Odysseus about the Sirens, Charybdis, and Scylla? How does Odysseus escape these terrible monsters?** Circe tells Odysseus that the Sirens use irresistibly beautiful voices to attract sailors, then attack and kill them. She gives him special wax to stop up his crew's ears. Then he has himself tied to the mast so that he can listen to the song without responding. Charybdis and Scylla are monsters who live in a narrow strait that Odysseus must pass through. Charybdis lives on the sea floor and sucks travelers into a terrible whirlpool. Scylla lives on the side of the cliff. She catches men and eats them with her six horrible heads. Odysseus loses six men to Scylla, but he and the rest of the crew go through the strait safely.

5. **Why does the ship stop at the sun god's island? Why do the men decide to kill some of his cattle in spite of the warnings? What are the consequences, for them and for Odysseus?** The ship returns to the sun god's island because a very strong wind blows them there. This wind keeps them from setting sail for many weeks until they have nothing to eat. The men kill some cattle because they think they have nothing to lose. They hope the gods may forgive them. Ironically, the winds change right away. When the crew tries to sail away, Zeus strikes their ship with a thunderbolt. All of them are killed except Odysseus. He clings to the mast and floats with the current for many days. He drifts ashore on the island of the nymph Calypso, who cares for him. She falls in love with him and keeps him with her for seven years.

6. **How does Odysseus finally reach Ithaca? Why does Athene come to him when he reaches land?** Ironically, Odysseus finally reaches Ithaca when Alcinous, who is a grandson of Poseidon, lends him a ship and crew to take him home. Once he reaches Ithaca, his patron goddess, Athene, is allowed to help him. She tells him again about the "guests" who are living in his palace and harassing his wife. She offers to disguise him as an old man and bring his son, Telemachus, to help him drive the unwanted guests away.

Informational Text Connections

Types of informational text with connections to these chapters include:

A news account of a recent shipwreck, storm at sea, or sea rescue
Travel brochures or magazine articles on modern-day Greece
Advertisements for Mediterranean Sea cruises

Select a text appropriate to your students' reading level and interests. Have them read and analyze the text using applicable criteria from the Common Core Standards. (Remember that different texts will lend themselves to different approaches for comprehension and analysis.)

 ## Literature-Related Writing

1. The Greeks imagined the mythical monsters Scylla and Charybdis in the narrow, dangerous strait between Italy and Sicily, which Greek sailors sometimes really had to navigate. Think of a dangerous place in your city or region. Write an **imaginative story** about a monster or monsters that might live there.

2. Suppose Odysseus had lived today. What dangers might he have had to face? Write a **modern version** retelling one episode of Odysseus' journey in a modern setting. (For example, you could make Odysseus a soldier trying to reach home after the war in Afghanistan or another recent conflict.)

3. Some of Odysseus' most frustrating setbacks came as a result of his men's mistakes (for example, setting the winds free when they were almost home, or killing some of the sun god's cattle). However, Odysseus blames himself as the leader for allowing these things to occur. Do you agree? Write a short **essay** defining true leadership as you understand it. Tell how much control you think a leader should exercise over his or her followers in different types of situations.

Extension Activities

1. Because some of the places mentioned are imaginary, there are different ways to map Odysseus' journey. Why not imagine a map of your own? Draw or trace an outline map of the Mediterranean world. Locate the places we can identify, such as Troy, Ithaca, Libya, and Sicily (Thrinacia). Using these places as landmarks, trace Odysseus' route as you imagine it. Label the places where you imagine each incident in the story occurring.

2. When Calypso finally allows Odysseus to leave her home, he has to make his own boat. Research how boats were made in the ancient world. Share what you learn with your class.

3. Draw or model one of the monsters that Odysseus encounters. Or, illustrate a scene from this section of the story.

Literature Test

1. **Odysseus' men make two important mistakes in this section of the story. What are they? What are the consequences of each of these mistakes?** The first important mistake is letting the winds out of the bag when the fleet first nears Ithaca. The consequence of this is that a terrible storm arises and blows the fleet back to where it came from. The second important mistake is killing some of the sun god's cattle on the island of Thrinacia. As a consequence, a thunderbolt strikes the one remaining ship, and all of the men except Odysseus himself are killed.

2. **What must Odysseus do in order for the ghosts in the land of the dead to speak with him? What does he learn from them?** In order for the ghosts to speak with Odysseus, he must let them drink the blood of the animals he has sacrificed. Students should mention at least one of the following pieces of information: Odysseus learns from the ghosts that his family is still waiting for him patiently, but that usurpers are eager to take his throne and his wife from him. He also receives a warning not to touch the herds of the sun god, for doing so would bring about swift and terrible judgment from the gods.

3. **Circe warns Odysseus about three terrible dangers that he must encounter: the Sirens, Scylla, and Charybdis. Describe at least two of these monsters.** The Sirens disguise themselves as beautiful women and lure sailors with their divinely lovely voices.

Then, they catch them and devour them. Scylla is a monster with six heads that lives on a cliff overlooking a narrow waterway. When boats go by, each head grabs a person to devour. Charybdis lives on the sea floor. She sucks entire boats into a powerful whirlpool, digests their crews, and spits back out what she has not managed to digest. (Students should describe at least two.)

4. **Two of the beautiful women who help Odysseus in the course of his journey are Circe, the powerful enchantress, and Calypso, the sea nymph who nurses him back to health after he has lost everything. In the Venn diagram given below, compare and contrast these two powerful women and Odysseus' experience with them.** Possible answers are shown. (Note: Students probably will not include all of these details. However, their answers should include at least two similarities and at least two differences.)

Circe

an enchantress who turns men into animals

tries to trick Odysseus at first

Odysseus stays with her willingly

lets Odysseus go when he asks her to

Both

beautiful

in love with Odysseus

want him to stay with them

offer him food, shelter, and help

Calypso

a sea nymph

nurses Odysseus to health when he washes up on her shore

Odysseus doesn't want to stay with her

makes him stay for 7 years, and only lets him go on Zeus's order

Discussion Guide #3

Chapters 11 - 17 (pages 62-96)

Vocabulary List A

overgrown (p. 62)	ambush (n., p. 66)	rival (n., p. 72)
myriad (adj., p. 62)	captivity (p. 68)	swaggered (p. 73)
succulent (p. 62)	languishes (p. 68)	gorging (p. 73)
*faltered (p. 62)	derision (p. 68)	raucous (p. 73)
treading (p. 62)	guile (p. 70)	vermin-infested (p. 74)
paddock (p. 62)	outwit (p. 71)	gleefully (p. 74)
dissolute (p. 63)	*pondering (p. 71)	degenerate (v., p. 76)
unsavory (p. 63)	*assent (n., p. 71)	cringing (p. 76)
scrounge (p. 63)	ruthless (p. 71)	parasite (p. 76)
suitors (p. 64)	effectively (p. 71)	bloated (p. 76)
penetrated (p. 64)	*contempt (p. 71)	uproar (p. 76)
*plight (p. 65)	bleak (p. 72)	commotion (p. 76)

Special Glossary

boar - savage wild pigs

hearth - the floor in front of a fireplace; the center of home and family life

Crete - (KREET) a large Mediterranean island nation south of Greece

Pylos - (PEE-lohss) a port city located on the west coast of the Peloponnese

Samos - (SAM-ohss) a large island near the coast of Turkey, used mistakenly here. This should probably be Cephalonia (Seff-uh-LOH-nee-yah), the large island just southwest of Ithaca

cove of Phorcys - (FOR-kiss) a cove on Ithaca's southern coast, sacred to the sea god Poseidon's father-in-law (page 58)

Zacynthus - (Za-KIN-thuss) a large island northwest of the Peloponnese

scythe - a farming tool used to cut grass or grain

plow - a farming tool used to turn and break up the earth for planting

Glossary of Starred Words

faltered - stumbled; fell; hesitated

plight - a difficult, unfortunate, or tragic situation

pondering - considering; reflecting; thinking about

assent - agreement

contempt - scorn; dislike; strong disapproval

Sample Meaningful Sentences for Starred Words

1. Maria felt so sick and weak that she **faltered** as she left the room, and we rushed to catch her so that she would not fall.

2. Everyone wanted to help when we heard about the **plight** of the families that lost their homes in the big earthquake.

3. Before she began to write her essay, Deirdre spent at least ten minutes **pondering** what she should write about.

4. When Jeff wants to borrow the car, Dad always asks where he's going and who he'll be with before giving his **assent** and handing him the keys.

5. Mr. Sloan has no patience with liars, so he didn't bother to hide his **contempt** when he discovered the cheaters' dishonesty.

The Writer's Craft

Metaphor

You might remember that **personification** is a figure of speech in which an inanimate object or an idea is compared to a person or given human characteristics. A **metaphor** is another important figure of speech. A metaphor states or suggests that one thing, person, or place actually *is* another thing. For example, we might read, "When Mrs. Jackson came in the house, the children peppered her with a volley of questions." This statement implies or suggests that the questions are bullets or balls that the children are throwing at the mother. It indicates that the children are throwing the questions out pell-mell, without even giving her a chance to answer; their mother feels bombarded when she hears all of the questions coming at her at once. When you read a metaphor, it is important to understand *what* two things are being compared, and *how* these things are alike.

This example is a simple metaphor. However, metaphors can also be *extended*. This means that the writer or speaker compares one situation to another showing several ways in which the two are similar. Suppose we read, "Although the children peppered her with a volley of questions, Mrs. Jackson threw up a shield of dignified silence and stalked into the kitchen." In this example, the metaphor has been extended. Instead of just one comparison (questions=bullets), there are now two related comparisons (questions=bullets, and dignified silence=a shield).

In the next section, Odysseus criticizes the unwelcome guests in his palace, speaking to them about dogs and a lion. Of course, Odysseus is not really speaking of animals; instead, this speech is an extended metaphor. Who or what is Odysseus comparing to dogs and a lion? What similarities does he suggest in speaking of them this way?

DISCUSSION QUESTIONS AND ACTIVITIES

Section I. Read chapters 11-13 (pages 62-76). Discuss answers to the following questions with a classmate, then write your answers separately.

1. **Why do you think Odysseus does not reveal his true identity to old Eumaeus** (You-MAY-us)**, the swineherd? What evidence does Eumaeus give of his loyalty and good character, even though he does not recognize Odysseus in his disguise?** Answers may vary as to why Odysseus does not reveal his true identity to the loyal swineherd. One possibility is that, despite Athene's assurances, he wants to test Eumaeus' loyalty for himself, and he wants to hear him speak freely, as he would to a stranger, in order to judge his true character. In addition, of course, Odysseus does not want news of his arrival on the island to become public knowledge: the fewer people one makes party to a secret, the better one's chances of keeping the secret. Finally, in keeping his identity a secret from Eumaeus, Odysseus is being obedient to Athene, who specifically instructed him to do so.

   Eumaeus' good character is obvious from the generous welcome he gives the "stranger," Odysseus. His complaints about the usurpers in Odysseus' palace show where his loyalties lie, as do his fond words about Odysseus and his hope that Odysseus may yet return.

2. **What characteristics can Odysseus see in his son, Telemachus, when he meets him at Eumaeus' house? Give evidence from the text to support your answer.** Odysseus can see that Telemachus is kind-hearted, generous, and respectful of his elders. This much is clear from the way he treats the "beggar" he meets at Eumaeus' house. At this point he is still fearful of the intruders in the palace. Also, he is wise and realistic in his evaluation; although he detests the suitors, he realizes that his mother will soon have to choose one of them, if only to clear the rest out of the palace.

3. **How do Telemachus' feelings about his situation change when he realizes that his father has returned? Who do Odysseus and Telemachus rely on to help them in their cause?** When Telemachus realizes that his father has returned, his fear of the suitors melts away. He feels much more courageous and is willing to challenge them. He and Odysseus are convinced that,

with Zeus's and Athene's help, they can overcome the intruders and restore the kingship.

4. **The would-be suitors in Odysseus' palace have already suffered one setback to their evil plans. What is it? What difference do they notice in Telemachus' behavior and attitude toward them?** The first setback to the suitors' evil plans is the fact that Telemachus arrived safely in Ithaca, escaping the ambush they had set up to kill him. The suitors also notice that Telemachus is bolder and more assertive than he has ever been before. When they threaten to throw the old beggar, who is really Odysseus in disguise, to the dogs, Telemachus puts his foot down and refuses to allow this injustice.

5. **Explain the extended metaphor that Odysseus, as the old beggar, uses to criticize the suitors. Who are the "dogs," and who is the "lion," in this metaphor? What point is he making?** The beggar tells the chief suitors that they think they are great because the other dogs submit to them. He implies that the chief suitors are the top dogs, and the lesser suitors are lower down in the hierarchy of the pack. He adds that when the lion returns to his lair, all of the dogs will die. The lion is of course Odysseus himself, and the lair is the palace. The implication is that Odysseus is as much greater, more powerful, and nobler than the suitors, as a lion is greater than dogs. Like cowardly dogs who make free in what they presume to be the abandoned lair of a lion, the suitors will face a deadly retribution when the legitimate lord of the habitation returns.

Make a
Prediction:

How will Odysseus make himself known to his wife, Penelope? How will he and Telemachus rid the palace of the would-be suitors?

Guided Discussion:

Discuss some of the key questions and activities in Section I. In addition, feel free to include in your discussion questions that are not in the Discussion Guide.

Vocabulary Prediction Check-up

Return to the vocabulary prediction chart, and use it to check the predictions students made prior to reading this section of the book. Remind students that, even if their predictions did not prove true, the value was in making them.

Vocabulary List B

tarnished (p. 77)	trance (p. 84)	harpooned (p. 91)
loathsome (p. 77)	whiled (p. 86)	*restrained (p. 92)
pathetic (p. 78)	supple (p. 86)	carnage (p. 92)
petty (p. 79)	humiliation (p. 87)	suspended (p. 93)
feat (p. 79)	*reprieve (p. 88)	rife (p. 94)
*conferring (p. 82)	*connoisseur (p. 88)	passionately (p. 94)
festive (p. 82)	veritable (p. 88)	declaimed (p. 94)
cronies (p. 83)	extension (p. 88)	scourge (p. 94)
coy (p. 83)	slavering (p. 89)	memorable (p. 96)
intervene (p. 84)	*obstinate (p. 90)	cherish (p. 96)
mesmerized (v., p. 84)	swathe (p. 90)	

Special Glossary

shroud - a burial cloth (Laertes is not yet dead, but he is a very old man)

Ilium - (ILL-ee-um) another name for Troy

archer - a person who shoots a bow and arrows

nurse - here, a nursemaid or nanny, who cares for a child from infancy

Parnassus - (Par-NASS-uss) a mountain in central Greece

missiles - here, objects that are thrown

quiverful - a quiver is a sheath used to hold arrows (see illustration in the book on page 85)

javelins - spears

Glossary of Starred Words

conferring - consulting together; discussing

reprieve - a postponement of an unpleasant event

connoisseur - an expert; someone who knows a subject well

obstinate - stubborn

restrained - held back

Sample Meaningful Sentences for Starred Words

1. The eighth-grade teachers were **conferring** with the music teacher about the plans for our field trip to the symphony.

2. We were supposed to present our oral reports today, but we got a **reprieve**; Ms. Harris said we could wait and do them Monday.

3. Mr. Gavotti was a great **connoisseur** of opera; he knew many works by heart and recognized the singers' voices with his eyes closed.

4. Arnold and his dad argue a lot because each is too **obstinate** to listen to the other, admit he might be wrong, or even consider changing his mind.

5. My dog wanted to jump up and lick the visitors in the face, but I **restrained** him because I knew this greeting would annoy them.

 The Writer's Craft

Climax and *Dénouement*

The **climax** of a story is the crisis or turning point that leads to a resolution of its conflict. Odysseus' conflict throughout the *Odyssey* has been the struggle to return to his home and his rightful place as king. What is the climax of the story? How does it lead to resolution of Odysseus' problems?

The word **dénouement** (day-noo-MANH) refers to the resolution of the conflict. What do you think of the dénouement of the *Odyssey*? Does it seem like a fairy-tale ending, like real life, or something in between?

DISCUSSION QUESTIONS AND ACTIVITIES

Section II. Read chapters 14-17 (pp. 77-96). Discuss answers to the following questions with a classmate, then write your answers separately.

1. **Why doesn't Odysseus tell Penelope right away who he really is? What does he learn from his conversation with her? How do he and Telemachus prepare to confront the suitors?** Odysseus doesn't tell Penelope right away who he really is because he is afraid it would be impossible for her to keep his arrival a secret. Odysseus knows that he needs the advantage of surprise if he and Telemachus are to overcome the many suitors; if the suitors found out about his arrival before the opportune moment, they would simply kill him quietly and deny that he had ever returned. Above all, Odysseus does not want Penelope to be disappointed yet again, as she would be if the suitors were to win the upcoming confrontation. Odysseus' conversation with Penelope is crucial to the plot, however; through it, he (and the reader) learn the test that will determine who is to have Penelope's hand in marriage. Odysseus and Telemachus prepare for the contest by removing the arms from the walls of the banquet hall and hiding their own weapons behind the door.

2. **How does Athene intervene when the suitors begin to mock Odysseus and defy Telemachus? How does this *foreshadow* or hint at the punishment they will soon receive?** Athene puts the arrogant suitors into a trance; they begin to laugh and cry uncontrollably as blood begins to trickle from the corners of their mouths. In addition, day turns to night and the meat on their plates begins to bleed. This foreshadows the coming judgment, when they will be caught in the grimace of death, their blood will flow freely, and they will be cast into everlasting night.

3. **Why does the news of Odysseus' return cause controversy (serious disagreement) in the city? Use the T-chart below to summarize the arguments of Eupeithes** (YOU-pith-eez, **Antinous' father) and of Halitherses** (Hal-ih-THUR-seez). **How is this disagreement resolved?** The news of Odysseus' return is controversial because it is accompanied by the news that he has killed over a hundred of the men of the city, stirring up fury and resentment among the relatives of the deceased. Possible answers for the T-chart are shown below.

Eupeithes' Position	Halitherses' Position
Odysseus led the young men of the city away to their death twenty years earlier; now he has slaughtered the suitors, a second generation.	The death of the second generation is actually the fault of the older Ithacans, who let them run wild and did not restrain them in their wrongdoing.
Odysseus, the bringer of death, should be punished by death, ridding the city of the ongoing danger he represents.	The gods, not Odysseus, decreed the death of these young men. There has been enough killing; now it is time to make peace.

This disagreement on policy is abruptly resolved when Eupeithes is struck by lightning (the preferred mode of punishment of Zeus himself) as he tries to attack Odysseus, a clear sign that Zeus is on Odysseus' side and that further combat is pointless. The goddess Athene then appears to the Ithacans and advises them to make their peace and move on with their lives.

Guided Discussion:

Discuss some of the key questions and activities in Section II. In addition, feel free to include in your discussion questions that are not in the Discussion Guide. Ask students to explain why, and how, Penelope verifies her husband's identity (pages 92-93).

Ask students to identify the **climax** of the story. The climax comes when Odysseus sends his arrow winging through the rings on the ax-handles, then throws off his disguise to challenge the usurpers openly.

Ask students to comment on the **dénouement** of the story, particularly on whether they find it realistic or otherwise. On one hand, the larger-than-life heroic figures and divinities obviously do not fit the category of realistic fiction. Point out, however, that there is a certain realism on a higher level, typified by the controversy surrounding Odysseus' dispatching of the suitors. This is not a fairy-tale, "everyone-lived-happily-ever-after," type of ending; instead, it recognizes that there is real tragedy, real pain, and potential conflict involved in the meting out of justice – but that a community can survive, and find a measure of joy, despite the pain.

You may or may not want to ask students to compare the reactions of the citizens of Ithaca to the suitors' death, to the response when lawbreakers are arrested or killed in their communities. Do people's responses vary, as did those of Eupeithes and Halitherses? How do students respond personally to these tragic situations?

 Vocabulary Prediction Check-up

Return to the vocabulary prediction chart, and use it to check the predictions students made prior to reading this section of the book. Remind students that, even if their predictions did not prove true, the value was in making them.

 Selection Review

1. **Odysseus' son Telemachus has grown to manhood while Odysseus was gone. How does Odysseus feel when he finally meets him? How does Odysseus' return change Telemachus' feelings about dealing with the would-be suitors?** Odysseus feels pleased and proud of his son because Telemachus is kind, generous, and respectful. Both father and son are also pleased because they look so much alike. Before his father's return, Telemachus was afraid to challenge the suitors. He thought his mother would just have to marry one of them so that the others would leave. However, Odysseus' return makes Telemachus feel braver. He stands up to the suitors and plots with his father to get rid of them completely.

2. **Who are the dogs, and who is the lion, in Odysseus' *extended metaphor*? Why does he make this comparison?** Odysseus compares the would-be suitors to a pack of dogs in an empty lion's den. The lion is Odysseus himself. Odysseus makes this comparison to show that the suitors are cowardly, second-rate men. They are trying to take the place of someone much greater and nobler than any of them. Just as a lion will destroy dogs that it finds in its den, Odysseus will destroy the suitors when he comes home.

3. **Why does Odysseus hide his identity from his wife, Penelope? Describe her plan for choosing a new husband. How will Odys-**

seus use this to reach his goal of getting rid of the suitors? Odysseus hides his identity from Penelope because he does not want to put her under the stress of keeping his secret. He also does not want to raise her hopes until he is sure that the suitors are out of the way. Penelope plans a contest to choose a new husband. She will ask the suitors to string Odysseus' bow, then shoot it with the kind of skill that Odysseus had. She will marry the one who can do this first. If none of them succeeds, she will marry the one who can at least string the bow. Odysseus realizes that none of the suitors will be able to handle his bow. He plans to show them up in the contest. Then he and Telemachus will challenge them openly.

4. **How does Odysseus prove his true identity? What happens to the suitors?** Of course, the suitors fail even to string Odysseus' bow. Odysseus is still disguised as a beggar. He strings the bow easily and sends the arrow through the rings. Then he and Telemachus challenge the suitors. The doors of the banquet hall are closed so they cannot escape. Odysseus, Telemachus, and the faithful swineherd Eumaeus defeat and kill all of the suitors.

5. **How does Penelope respond when she hears that her husband has returned? How does she find out whether he is truly Odysseus?** When Penelope hears that Odysseus is back, at first she thinks it is too good to be true. Even when she sees the old scar on his leg, she is afraid a god in disguise is testing her faithfulness to her husband. She tests him by pretending that she had their bed moved out of their room. Odysseus angrily replies that the bed was too big to be removed from the room unless it was cut in pieces. Then Penelope knows that he really is her husband.

6. **Why are some of the townspeople angry about Odysseus' return? Why does this cause disagreement? How is the situation finally resolved?** Some of the townspeople are angry about Odysseus' return because they are relatives or friends of the suitors he killed. They say that he brings nothing but death, and they want to punish him with death. However, other townspeople say that the suitors died because they were greedy, dishonest, and out of control. They say that the older people in town are to blame, because they did not teach these young men to behave responsibly. They say that their deaths were a judgment from the gods. The angry citizens try to attack Odysseus. Then Zeus, king of the gods, strikes their leader with lightning. The goddess Athene appears and tells the people to forgive and live in peace.

Informational Text Connections

Types of informational text with connections to this section include:

Accounts of modern-day soldiers designated as MIA (missing in action), for example during the Vietnam War, or POWs (prisoners of war) returning home after a number of years

Information on archery as a sport

Select a text appropriate to your students' reading level and interests. Have them read and analyze the text using applicable criteria from the Common Core Standards. (Remember that different texts will lend themselves to different approaches for comprehension and analysis.)

 Literature-Related Writing

1. Pretend you are Telemachus or Penelope. Write two or three **journal entries** describing your feeling about the events described in this section.

2. The movie *O Brother, Where Art Thou?* is a loose modern retelling of the *Odyssey*. With a parent's permission, view this movie as a DVD. Write a **review** of the movie in which you compare and contrast it with the classic *Odyssey* story.

3. Fatalism, the belief that people's lives are ruled by a destiny they cannot escape, is an important part of the *Odyssey*'s perspective on the world. When the gods are against Odysseus, it is impossible for him to succeed; then, when the gods are on his side, it is impossible for him to fail. What do you think of this idea? Which is more important: outside forces beyond a person's control, or the person's own choices and decisions? Write an **essay** stating your point of view. Support your argument with examples from real life.

Extension Activities

1. Make a model or diorama of Odysseus' palace.

2. With a parent's permission, view the movie *O Brother, Where Art Thou?,* a loose modern retelling of the *Odyssey* story (see Literature-Related Writing #2, *above*). Discuss with your classmates the similarities and differences between the movie and the book.

3. Draw or paint a picture an illustration for this part of the book, *or* design and create an original cover for the book.

Literature Test

1. What change do the suitors notice in Telemachus after he meets Odysseus? Why do you think this change occurs? After Telemachus meets his father, he no longer fears the suitors as he did before. He stands up to them and challenges them when they are disorderly and cruel. His father's presence gives Telemachus new courage. He also believes that the gods are on his side, and he realizes that there is no question of Penelope choosing one of the suitors as a husband now that Odysseus is back.

2. Explain thoroughly Odysseus' metaphor of the dogs and the lion. How does Odysseus' prediction come true? Odysseus compares the suitors to a pack of cowardly dogs who have taken over a lion's den. He compares himself, Odysseus, to the lion. Odysseus wants to show that he is much greater and nobler than the suitors, just as a lion is greater and nobler than a dog. Also, he predicts that when the lion returns to its den, he will destroy the dogs. This prediction of the suitors' fate comes true when Odysseus challenges and kills them.

3. How does Penelope plan to choose a new husband? What happens at the contest? Penelope plans a contest to choose a new husband. To win, a suitor must string Odysseus' old bow and shoot it as skillfully as Odysseus used to do. If no one succeeds, then the first to string the bow will become her husband. However, when the contest takes place, none of the suitors can even string the bow. Only the old beggar, Odysseus himself, succeeds in stringing the bow and shooting it. Then he reveals his identity and kills his rivals.

4. **Explain the trouble that arises when the townspeople hear what happened at the palace. How is this trouble resolved?**
When the townspeople hear what happened, many of them are very angry, because they are relatives or friends of the men who were killed. They want to attack and kill Odysseus. Others, however, blame the men's deaths on the town's failure to keep them in check and the decision of the gods to punish them. Resolution is swift when the fractious party moves to attack Odysseus: Zeus strikes their leader with lightning. The goddess Athene appears and enjoins the people to forgive and to build their lives in peace.

Selection Review #1

The Odyssey

Chapters 1 - 5

1. **Who is Odysseus? What do we learn from these chapters about his past?** Odysseus, the king of the small Greek island of Ithaca, is also a military leader and hero. We learn that he left his home twenty years earlier to lead troops in the Greeks' war against the city of Troy. The war went on for ten years before the Greeks finally won. However, Odysseus did not succeed in returning to his home when the war was over. He has been wandering around the Mediterranean Sea for the past ten years. He has suffered a great deal during that time.

2. **How does Odysseus arrive at King Alcinous' court? What makes King Alcinous and his nobles realize that Odysseus is an unusual and important person?** Odysseus was drawing near Ithaca, his island home, when a terrible storm tipped his boat over. Odysseus was thrown into the water. He had to swim for his life. He finally washed up on the shore of Phaeicia. Nausicaa, the daughter of the king of Phaeicia, gave him food and clothing and took him to her father's court. King Alcinous and his nobles realized that Odysseus was an unusual and important person when he threw the discus farther than their champion athletes. They also noticed him weeping as he listened to their court singer telling the stories of the Trojan War, so they guessed that he had something to do with that war.

3. **What are some of the good qualities that made Odysseus such a hero to the Greeks? Give some examples from the text.** First, Odysseus is a clever, intelligent leader. For example, he thought up the trick with the wooden horse that helped the Greeks win the Trojan War. He also thought up a clever plan to trick the Cyclops when he and his men were trapped in the giant's cave. Second, Odysseus is very brave. He led his men in the attack on Troy. He also led the plan to blind the Cyclops and escape from him. Finally, Odysseus is patient. He waited patiently in the wooden horse until night when he and his men could come out. He has been trying to reach home for ten years, but he still has not given up hope.

4. **What are some of Odysseus' weak points? What are some of the consequences he has suffered because of his mistakes?** One of Odysseus' weak points is that he does not exercise leadership to make his men do what is right. Instead, he often goes along with them, even when he knows that what they are doing is wrong. For example, he took part in the terrible killing at Troy. The Greeks killed old people, women, and children as well as soldiers. Afterward, they attacked Ismarus for no reason at all. They again killed innocent people and looted their goods. Odysseus knew this was wrong, but he did not stop his men. Then, he knew they should leave before the townspeople came back. Instead, he let his men talk him into staying on the beach and partying all night. They were attacked at dawn and several men were killed.

continued...

Odysseus' greatest fault, however, is his pride. His pride leads him to tell the Cyclops his real name as he escapes. The Cyclops curses him, calling on the sea god Poseidon to ruin his trip and keep him from reaching home safely. This curse leads to all of Odysseus' later troubles.

5. **What do we learn from this text about the Greeks' view of the gods? What role do gods, goddesses, and other supernatural beings play in Odysseus' adventures?** We see in the text that the gods and goddesses were very important in the Greeks' view of life. They believed that the gods could be jealous or moody, and that they acted directly in people's affairs. For example, when Odysseus senses danger, he asks the goddess Athena to help him. All his troubles occur because the god Poseidon is angry with him. When he is shipwrecked, he survives because a sea nymph, Ino, gives him good advice, as well as a magic scarf to help him swim to shore.

Selection Review #2

The Odyssey

Chapters 6 - 10

1. **Aeolus tries to help Odysseus reach home. What goes wrong? What happens to most of Odysseus' ships and men?** Aeolus ties three of the winds in a bag, so that only the west wind is free to blow the fleet to Ithaca. He tells Odysseus to make sure the bag remains closed until they reach home. Unfortunately, Odysseus falls asleep once they are in sight of Ithaca. His men open the bag, and the other winds blow up a storm, driving the fleet back to Aeolus' island. Aeolus refuses to help them again. The fleet drifts around until it reaches a harbor. The giants who live there crush the ships and eat their crews. Only Odysseus' ship and its crew escape disaster.

2. **How does Circe trick the men? What changes this situation? What is *ironic* about what happens next?** Circe puts drugs in the drinks she offers Odysseus' men. Then she changes them into pigs. When Odysseus hears about this, he wants to rescue his men. The god Hermes gives him a plant to help him resist Circe's magic. Odysseus forces her to change his men back. Ironically, once Circe stops putting spells on the men, she offers them a warm welcome. She offers to make love to Odysseus. He agrees, and the men stay in her palace for about a year.

3. **Why does Odysseus sacrifice sheep when he visits the land of the dead? What useful information does he learn from the ghosts?** Odysseus sacrifices sheep so the ghosts can drink their blood. The warm blood gives the ghosts enough life to see Odysseus and talk with him for a short time. One of the ghosts, Tiresias, is an old prophet. He warns Odysseus about the dangers of his journey. He especially warns against killing any of the sun god's cattle. He tells Odysseus that unwanted guests in his palace want to become king in his place. Another ghost is Odysseus' mother. She tells him that his father, his wife, and his son are still alive. His wife still waits for him faithfully, but she is having trouble with unwanted guests.

4. **What does Circe tell Odysseus about the Sirens, Charybdis, and Scylla? How does Odysseus escape these terrible monsters?** Circe tells Odysseus that the Sirens use irresistibly beautiful voices to attract sailors, then attack and kill them. She gives him special wax to stop up his crew's ears. Then he has himself tied to the mast so that he can listen to the song without responding. Charybdis and Scylla are monsters who live in a narrow strait that Odysseus must pass through. Charybdis lives on the sea floor and sucks travelers into a terrible whirlpool. Scylla lives on the side of the cliff. She catches men and eats them with her six horrible heads. Odysseus loses six men to Scylla, but he and the rest of the crew go through the strait safely.

continued...

5. **Why does the ship stop at the sun god's island? Why do the men decide to kill some of his cattle in spite of the warnings? What are the consequences, for them and for Odysseus?** The ship returns to the sun god's island because a very strong wind blows them there. This wind keeps them from setting sail for many weeks until they have nothing to eat. The men kill some cattle because they think they have nothing to lose. They hope the gods may forgive them. Ironically, the winds change right away. When the crew tries to sail away, Zeus strikes their ship with a thunderbolt. All of them are killed except Odysseus. He clings to the mast and floats with the current for many days. He drifts ashore on the island of the nymph Calypso, who cares for him. She falls in love with him and keeps him with her for seven years.

6. **How does Odysseus finally reach Ithaca? Why does Athene come to him when he reaches land?** Ironically, Odysseus finally reaches Ithaca when Alcinous, who is a grandson of Poseidon, lends him a ship and crew to take him home. Once he reaches Ithaca, his patron goddess, Athene, is allowed to help him. She tells him again about the "guests" who are living in his palace and harassing his wife. She offers to disguise him as an old man and bring his son, Telemachus, to help him drive the unwanted guests away.

Selection Review #3

The Odyssey

Chapters 11 - 17

1. **Odysseus' son Telemachus has grown to manhood while Odysseus was gone. How does Odysseus feel when he finally meets him? How does Odysseus' return change Telemachus' feelings about dealing with the would-be suitors?** Odysseus feels pleased and proud of his son because Telemachus is kind, generous, and respectful. Both father and son are also pleased because they look so much alike. Before his father's return, Telemachus was afraid to challenge the suitors. He thought his mother would just have to marry one of them so that the others would leave. However, Odysseus' return makes Telemachus feel braver. He stands up to the suitors and plots with his father to get rid of them completely.

2. **Who are the dogs, and who is the lion, in Odysseus' *extended metaphor*? Why does he make this comparison?** Odysseus compares the would-be suitors to a pack of dogs in an empty lion's den. The lion is Odysseus himself. Odysseus makes this comparison to show that the suitors are cowardly, second-rate men. They are trying to take the place of someone much greater and nobler than any of them. Just as a lion will destroy dogs that it finds in its den, Odysseus will destroy the suitors when he comes home.

3. **Why does Odysseus hide his identity from his wife, Penelope? Describe her plan for choosing a new husband. How will Odysseus use this to reach his goal of getting rid of the suitors?** Odysseus hides his identity from Penelope because he does not want to put her under the stress of keeping his secret. He also does not want to raise her hopes until he is sure that the suitors are out of the way. Penelope plans a contest to choose a new husband. She will ask the suitors to string Odysseus' bow, then shoot it with the kind of skill that Odysseus had. She will marry the one who can do this first. If none of them succeeds, she will marry the one who can at least string the bow. Odysseus realizes that none of the suitors will be able to handle his bow. He plans to show them up in the contest. Then he and Telemachus will challenge them openly.

4. **How does Odysseus prove his true identity? What happens to the suitors?** Of course, the suitors fail even to string Odysseus' bow. Odysseus is still disguised as a beggar. He strings the bow easily and sends the arrow through the rings. Then he and Telemachus challenge the suitors. The doors of the banquet hall are closed so they cannot escape. Odysseus, Telemachus, and the faithful swineherd Eumaeus defeat and kill all of the suitors.

continued...

5. **How does Penelope respond when she hears that her husband has returned? How does she find out whether he is truly Odysseus?** When Penelope hears that Odysseus is back, at first she thinks it is too good to be true. Even when she sees the old scar on his leg, she is afraid a god in disguise is testing her faithfulness to her husband. She tests him by pretending that she had their bed moved out of their room. Odysseus angrily replies that the bed was too big to be removed from the room unless it was cut in pieces. Then Penelope knows that he really is her husband.

6. **Why are some of the townspeople angry about Odysseus' return? Why does this cause disagreement? How is the situation finally resolved?** Some of the townspeople are angry about Odysseus' return because they are relatives or friends of the suitors he killed. They say that he brings nothing but death, and they want to punish him by death. However, other townspeople say that the suitors died because they were greedy, dishonest, and out of control. They say that the older people in town are to blame, because they did not teach these young men to behave responsibly. They say that their deaths were a judgment from the gods. The angry citizens try to attack Odysseus. Then Zeus, king of the gods, strikes their leader with lightning. The goddess Athene appears and tells the people to forgive and live in peace.

Name: _____

Literature Test #1

The Odyssey

Chapters 1 - 5

1. Who is Odysseus? How does he come to be at King Alcinous' court in Phaeicia?

_____

_____

_____

_____

_____

_____

_____

2. One of Odysseus' strong points is his cleverness. Tell how Odysseus' cleverness helped him, both in ending the Trojan War and in escaping from the Cyclops.

_____

_____

_____

_____

_____

_____

_____

continued...

3. List two of Odysseus' weaknesses as a leader. Explain how each of these weaknesses caused trouble for Odysseus and his men.

_____

_____

_____

_____

_____

_____

_____

_____

4. How are the gods and goddesses involved in Odysseus' life? Give at least two specific examples.

_____

_____

_____

_____

_____

_____

_____

Name: _____

Literature Test #2

The Odyssey

Chapters 6 - 10

1. Odysseus' men make two important mistakes in this section of the story. What are they? What are the consequences of each of these mistakes?

_____

_____

_____

_____

_____

_____

_____

2. What must Odysseus do in order for the ghosts in the land of the dead to speak with him? What does he learn from them?

_____

_____

_____

_____

_____

_____

_____

continued...

3. Circe warns Odysseus about three terrible dangers that he must encounter: the Sirens, Charybdis, and Scylla. Describe each of these monsters.

_____

_____

_____

_____

_____

_____

_____

4. Two os the beautiful women who help Odysseus in the course of his journey are Circe, the powerful enchantress, and Calypso, the sea nymph who nurses him back to health after he has lost everything. In the Venn diagram given below, compare and contrast these two powerful women and Odysseus' experience with them.

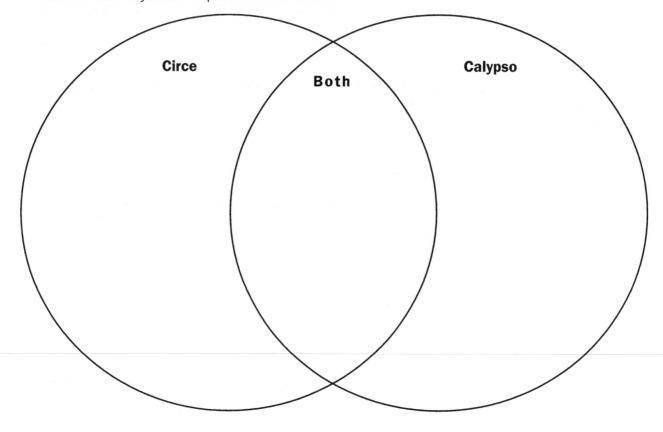

Circe　　　**Both**　　　**Calypso**

Name: _____

Literature Test #3

The Odyssey

Chapters 11 - 17

1. What change do the suitors notice in Telemachus after he meets Odysseus? Why do you think this change occurs?

    _____

    _____

    _____

    _____

    _____

    _____

2. Explain thoroughly Odysseus' metaphor of the dogs and the lion. How does Odysseus' prediction come true?

    _____

    _____

    _____

    _____

    _____

    _____

continued...

3. How does Penelope plan to choose a new husband? What happens at the contest?

_____

_____

_____

_____

_____

_____

_____

4. Explain the trouble that arises when the townspeople hear what happened at the palace. How is this trouble resolved?

_____

_____

_____

_____

_____

_____

_____

Name: _____

Vocabulary Test #1

The Odyssey

Chapters 1 - 5

WRITE MEANINGFUL SENTENCES FOR THE FOLLOWING WORDS:

oblivious	sumptuous	exuberant
makeshift	distress	despondent
ordeal	replenish	dissuade
	complacent	

_____

_____

_____

_____

_____

_____

_____

_____

_____

_____

_____

_____

_____

_____

Talent Development Secondary Program

Name: _____

Vocabulary Test #2

The Odyssey

Chapters 6 - 10

WRITE MEANINGFUL SENTENCES FOR THE FOLLOWING WORDS:

subdued	sensation	impending
anticipation	recognition	exertions
alternative	treacherous	regained
	unscathed	

_____

_____

_____

_____

_____

_____

_____

_____

_____

_____

_____

_____

_____

_____

Name: _____

Vocabulary Test #3

The Odyssey

Chapters 11 - 17

WRITE MEANINGFUL SENTENCES FOR THE FOLLOWING WORDS:

faltered	assent	connoisseur
plight	contempt	obstinate
pondering	conferring	restrained
	reprieve	

_____

_____

_____

_____

_____

_____

_____

_____

_____

_____

_____

_____

_____

_____

_____

Student Team Literature Discussion Guides are available for the following titles:

Non-fiction

The Acorn People

Anne Frank: The Diary of a Young Girl

Barack Obama: President for a New Era

Barack Obama: United States President

The Double Life of Pocahontas

First They Killed My Father

Freedom Train

Freedom's Children

Leon's Story

One More River to Cross: the Stories of Twelve Black Americans

Warriors Don't Cry

We Beat the Street

What's the Big Idea, Ben Franklin?

Short Stories, Poetry, and Mythology

Beowulf: A New Telling

The Dark-Thirty: Southern Tales of the Supernatural

A Dime a Dozen

The Dream Keeper and Other Poems

ego-tripping and other poems for young people

Keeping the Night Watch

The Library Card

Locomotion

Make Lemonade

The Odyssey, retold by Robin Lister

Novels

The Big Wave

Bridge to Terabithia

Bud, Not Buddy

The Bully

Call It Courage

The Call of the Wild

The Cay

Crash

Curse of a Winter Moon

Darnell Rock Reporting

A Day No Pigs Would Die

Eddie's Ordeal

Esperanza Rising

Fast Sam, Cool Clyde, and Stuff

Freak the Mighty

The Giver

Hatchet

The Hobbit

Holes

In the Night, on Lanvale Street

Jacob Have I Loved

Johnny Tremain

Journey

Justin and the Best Biscuits in the World

M. C. Higgins the Great

Maniac Magee

The Midwife's Apprentice

Monster

The Mystery of Apartment A-13

Ninjas, Piranhas, and Galileo

Nothing But the Truth

Number the Stars

The Outsiders

The Pinballs

Roll of Thunder, Hear My Cry

Sing Down the Moon

The Skin I'm In

To Kill a Mockingbird

Touching Spirit Bear

Tuck Everlasting

The Watsons Go to Birmingham—1963

The Westing Game

The Whipping Boy

Wringer

A Wrinkle in Time

Yolonda's Genius

For a catalog and ordering information, call 410-516-4339
For information on Student Team Literature professional development,
call Maria Waltemeyer (410-516-2247)
or visit the Talent Development Secondary website at
www.talentdevelopmentsecondary.com

Made in the USA
Las Vegas, NV
07 October 2021

31944861R00044